D1484162

TRUE UFO
ACCOUNTS

About the Author

David Godwin (Lakeville, Minnesota) is the managing editor of *FATE* magazine. He holds a Bachelor of Journalism degree from the University of Texas at Austin and is a student of esoteric lore, magic, and the Cabala.

COMPILED BY DAVID GODWIN

TRUE UFO
ACCOUNTS
FROM THE VAULTS OF FATE MAGAZINE

60 YEARS OF CLOSE ENCOUNTERS

Llewellyn Publications
Woodbury, Minnesota

First Edition
First Printing, 2011

Book design by Steffani Sawyer
Book edited by Ed Day
Cover design by Kevin R. Brown
Cover image courtesy of *FATE* magazine

Library of Congress Cataloging-in-Publication Data
True UFO accounts : from the vaults of Fate magazine : 60 years of close
encounters / compiled by David Godwin. — 1st ed.
     p. cm.
   ISBN 978-0-7387-2575-8
1. Unidentified flying objects. 2. Human-alien encounters. I. Godwin,
David. II. Fate (Chicago, Ill.)
   TL789.T825 2011
   001.942—dc23

                                                2011013579

Llewellyn Publications
A Division of Llewellyn Worldwide Ltd.
2143 Wooddale Drive
Woodbury, MN 55125-2989
www.llewellyn.com

Printed in the United States of America

CONTENTS

ix

INTRODUCTION

In July 1947, the modern UFO era began with the Kenneth Arnold sighting of nine strange flying objects in the mountains of Washington. He said that the objects moved in a peculiar fashion, like "saucers skipping on the water." The newspapers seized on this description, and the term "flying saucer" was born. And then everyone began seeing them, and reports poured into the Air Force from all over the country, and beyond.

In the summer of 1948, the first issue of FATE magazine was published. On the cover was a painting of Arnold's plane and a huge flying saucer. Inside was Arnold's own account of the incident.

Since then, UFO reports have continued to appear in the pages of FATE and are still doing so 63 years later. Flying saucers formed a large part of the content for many years, and although the emphasis of the magazine later grew to include ghosts, mediums, Bigfoot, and other paranormal events, it never lost sight of its heritage—the as-yet unexplained flying disk in the heavens.

As a teenager, I devoured Desmond Leslie and George Adamski's *Flying Saucers Have Landed* (1953). Most of the book was taken up by Leslie's history of the UFO phenomena, and here I learned about the vimana aircraft of ancient India and building the pyramids of Egypt with a flute. As for Adamski's personal account, I believed every word. How could I not? An encounter with a flying saucer by a scoutmaster was even written up in the prestigious mainstream *Boys' Life* magazine, which included a form to fill out if you saw a UFO. I read everything about flying saucers that I could get my hands on.

The phenomenon was being investigated by some rather prominent and respected people: J. Allen Hynek was hired by the Air Force to investigate and debunk, yet became convinced that he was dealing with something more than swamp gas. Frank Scully wrote several somewhat sensational books about crashed saucers, but nuclear physicist Stanton Friedman took the idea seriously enough to delve deeply into the Roswell event and made it a historical landmark. In France, Aimé Michel took a serious and scientific approach and became a staunch supporter of UFO reality. Gray Barker was somewhat of a jokester, and put over a few hoaxes, including the mysterious Men-in-Black, who later took on a reality of their own. Barker's investigation of the Flatwoods Monster may have inspired John Keel to go after Mothman in West Virginia.

Hundreds, thousands of people were seeing mysterious things in the sky. Not just lights, but metallic disks, cigars, and flying machines. Every now and then, there would be a close contact. But even more fascinating were the intimate contacts with the pilots and crew of these extraterrestrial spacecraft: the kindly Venusians who took Adamski on a tour of the solar system, or the less kindly nightmarish monsters with acid tentacles who stopped cars on lonely roads in West Virginia.

I liked the Venusians better. The eight-foot-tall slithering horrors were too frightening.

I read several books by Donald E. Keyhoe, which convinced me that Flying Saucers Are Real and that the government is Covering-Up. Not much has changed in that regard. I read Gerald Heard's bizarre theory that the aliens must be insects—bees, in all probability—in order to withstand the accelerations and sudden directional changes exhibited by their spacecraft.

I didn't read the skeptical material by astronomer Donald Menzel and other close-minded "enemies of truth." I didn't want to hear it.

I was enthralled. In any remote area, I would sit on the ground and wait, hoping an Adamski saucer would land and take me for a ride to a better and more fascinating world.

Unfortunately, or fortunately, that never happened—that I can remember.

Decades passed, UFOs ceased to be newsworthy, and then it quit being fun.

It had its beginning with the eight-foot octopoid monsters, but now it was worse than brief encounters and being badly scared.

Instead of taking people on nice pleasure excursions, the ETs were suddenly abducting people—by the thousands, evidently—and performing hideous experiments on them that left them scarred for life, physically and mentally. What made the aliens turn mean?

Some of them were reptiles who could disguise themselves as human. Others were giant praying mantises. Ick. What happened to the nice Venusians?

And then the legends of underground bases where repulsive ETs were allowed to perform Nazi medical experiment on human beings in return for snippets of alien technology. You know, like the cell phone or iPod. We let them mutilate cattle and gave them the Tesla death ray in return for the secrets of the Pentium microprocessor.

It isn't much fun anymore. Things have gotten so bad that I'm anxiously waiting for those nice Venusians to give me a ride out of here!

Yet after all this time, we still don't know what they really are. Spacecraft? Time machines from the future? Visitors from another dimension? According to some, the government knows but isn't telling. Or do they? Maybe all they are covering up is the fact that they know UFOs exist, but they haven't a clue as to what they are.

Because they haven't gone away. They're still being seen, frequently—swooping over Crawfordville, Texas; hovering over Chicago's O'Hare Airport; illuminating Mexican skies. They're everywhere.

As you will discover in the following pages, FATE has been along for the ride, all the way, informing, entertaining, enlightening.

—DAVID F. GODWIN

ONE: Prehistory

Strange things have been seen in the sky since ancient times, and probably before, but the modern UFO phenomenon really began with Kenneth Arnold's sighting of unidentified flying objects near Mt. Rainier in July 1947. Arnold's estimates of their speed ruled out the possibility that they were conventional aircraft. But what were they Arnold's sighting was very far from being the first time that anyone had ever looked up into the skies and seen something unusual, something they could not identify—or something that shouldn't have been there.

Quite aside from legendary flying craft such as the *vimana* sky chariots of India, there have been sightings of what we would now call "flying saucers" from earliest times. One of the best known such incidents was in AD 840, when Bishop Agobard of Lyon reported the attempted stoning of three strangers from "Magonia" who had fallen from a "cloud ship." Typical of these old accounts is that of a huge, long fiery object seen flying along a lake in Flüelen, Switzerland, in 1619. And the sightings have never stopped.

Reproduced here are stories of a UFO sighting in 1865 and of the well-known airship flap of 1897. UFOs are not a recent phenomena, which rules out the theory that they are all conventional aircraft or secret weapons of a terrestrial power.

The UFO Crash of 1865
By J. D. Haines

March-April 2009

General Robert E. Lee surrendered the Army of Northern Virginia to General Ulysses S. Grant on April 9, 1865. The same year, the first crash of an unidentified flying object (UFO) was reported in the western United States. The eyewitness account, provided by a trapper named James Lumley in present-day Montana, was widely circulated in the newspapers of the day.

Lumley's sighting predates the generally accepted 1947 inauguration of flying saucers in Roswell, New Mexico, by over 80 years, making it by far the oldest documented UFO crash. After the 1865 report, sightings of mysterious airships peaked in 1897, six years before the Wright Brothers flew at Kitty Hawk.

W. Ritchie Benedict, writing in FATE magazine, reported finding Lumley's story in two Canadian newspapers published in 1865. These papers claimed to be reprinting a story from the Missouri Democrat entitled:

An Extraordinary Story

A Meteoric Shower

Crockery Failing from the Sky

Mr. James Lumley, an old Rocky Mountain trapper, who has been stopping at the Everett House for several days, makes a most remarkable statement to us, and one which, if authenticated, will produce the greatest excitement in the scientific world. Mr. Lumley states that about the middle of last September, he was engaged in trapping in the mountains about seventy-five or one hundred miles from the Great Falls of the Upper Missouri, and in the neighborhood of what is known as Cadotte Pass. After sunset one evening, he beheld a bright luminous body in the heavens, which moved with great rapidity in an easterly direction. Visible for at least five seconds, when it suddenly separated into particles, resembling, Mr. Lumley describes it, "the bursting of a skyrocket in the air." A few minutes later, he heard a heavy explosion, which jarred the earth perceptibly, and this was shortly followed by a rushing sound, like a tornado sweeping through the forest. A strong wind sprang up about the same time, but suddenly subsided. Filling the air with peculiar odors of a sulphurous [sic] nature. These incidents would make a slight impression on the mind of Mr. Lumley, but for the fact that on the ensuing day he discovered, at the distance of about two miles from his camping place, he could see in either direction a wide path had been cut through the forest. Giant trees [were] uprooted and broke off near the ground. The tops of hills [were] shaved off and the earth plowed up in many places. Great and widespread havoc [was] everywhere visible. Following up this track of desolation, he soon ascertained the cause of it in the shape of an immense stone driven into the side of a mountain. The most remarkable part of the story is an examination of this stone and how it had been divided into compartments. In several places it was carved with hieroglyphics. Mr. Lumley also discovered fragments of a substance resembling glass, and here and there dark stains, as though caused by a liquid. He is confident that the hieroglyphics are the work of human hands, and the stone itself, is a fragment of an immense body, [which] must have [been] used for some purpose by animated beings.

Strange as this story appears, Mr. Lumley relates it with so much sincerity that we are forced to accept it as true. It is evident that the stone which he discovered is a fragment of the meteor that was visible in this section last September. The stone will be remembered in Leavenworth, Galena, and in this city by Col. Bonneville. At Leavenworth the stone separated into particles and exploded.

Astronomers have long held that it is probable that the heavenly bodies are inhabited—even the comets—and it may be that meteors are also. Meteors could be used as a conveyance by the inhabitants of other planets exploring space, and it may be that hereafter some future Columbus, from Mercury or Uranus, may land on this planet by means of a meteoric conveyance, and take possession thereof—as did the Spanish navigators of the New World in 1492, and eventually drive what is known as the 'human race' into a condition of the most abject servitude. There must be a race superior to us, and this may at some future time be demonstrated in the manner we have indicated.

While the conclusion of this story may sound quaint, with its references to aliens traveling through space on comets and meteors, there was the cult a few years back that committed mass suicide in order to catch a ride on a comet passing near the Earth. And there are undoubtedly still believers today.

Even though Lumley reported no evidence of survivors, the story implies the possibility. It would seem rather unlikely that a Rocky Mountain trapper would recognize hieroglyphics. It is equally doubtful that an advanced alien civilization would have developed a written language identical to man's hieroglyphics. Unless of course one accepts the premise that aliens visited Egypt and built the pyramids and gave the natives hieroglyphics.

Lumley's account sounds very much like a large meteorite striking the earth: a bright body moving rapidly through the darkened sky, breaking apart into particles, jarring the ground on impact, and cutting a path of destruction through the forest before imbedding itself in the side of a mountain.

Iron meteorites often appear pitted, or compartmentalized, as Lumley's story suggests. These pits are due to rust and atmospheric friction. Iron meteorites also may contain sulfur, accounting for the odor described by Lumley. Since meteorites heat up to several thousand degrees as they pass through the Earth's atmosphere, it would not be unusual to find elements in the Earth's surface where the meteorite struck heated enough to form obsidian, a form of natural glass.

In an article by Dan Ahrens in 1999, he points out that the modern reports of the supposed crash in Missouri are false. As he states, "The old article clearly states that Mr.

Lumley was in the Upper Missouri, which is of course located in Montana, and that he was 75 to 100 miles up from the Great Falls. This area is exactly where Cadotte Pass is located, so his recollection was very good as he reported it."

Ahrens also points out the newspaper's erroneous attempt to tie Lumley's meteorite to sightings in Leavenworth and Galena, Kansas. Unfortunately, Mr. Ahrens believes that a "craft," rather than a meteorite, crashed at the site. He further encourages the private sector to mount an investigation of the area, before "all traces just get whisked off to a government facility somewhere … never to be seen again." An investigation would be most welcome, as a museum-quality meteorite could be discovered. This would at least disprove the hieroglyphics claim.

So what are we make of this incredible tale? Just that— it was a tale, and a tall one at that. If Lumley witnessed anything, it was undoubtedly an enormous meteorite. But rather than cast aspersions upon Lumley's good name, it was likely a practical joker in the newspaper business that was responsible.

Newspapers of the latter part of the 19th century could be notoriously unreliable. Some of the first livestock mutilation cases were reported in Kansas in 1897. One incident, complete with a "cigar-shaped airship" with "strange beings" aboard that abducted a cow then dumped the mutilated carcass, turned out to a hoax propagated by a local Liar's Club, of whom the newspaper editor was a member.

Practical jokers abounded during the mysterious airship sightings of 1897, sending lighted kites aloft at night. Today there are so many UFO sightings that it is impossible to explain them all. Even so, it does not increase the likelihood that we have been visited by aliens who communicate with hieroglyphics and travel on meteors.

The Airships of 1897
By J. Allan Danelek

July 2007

Many people regard the Kenneth Arnold sighting of several flying disks over Mount Rainier in 1947 to be the official start of the modern age of ufology, but that would be incorrect. Actually, it all started earlier than that—almost 50 years earlier, in fact—with the airship flap of 1896–97, which to this day remains one of the most controversial elements of the entire UFO debate.

For those unfamiliar with this brief but curious incident (or series of incidents, as the sightings lasted several months), it all started on the evening of November 17, 1896, when a bright light appeared through the dark rainclouds over Sacramento, California, and slowly made its way westward over the capitol building, only to disappear once again into the night—leaving hundreds of the cities' residents wondering what they had just witnessed. It was described by various witnesses as "cigar shaped" and reportedly sported oversized propellers and rudders on its undercarriage, all visible due to its low altitude and slow progress. Among those who saw the vessel was an assistant to the Secretary of State, who, along with several friends, watched the vessel for several minutes from the capitol dome. One person even described it as having wheels at its side "like the side wheels on Fulton's old steamboat."

The mysterious object was seen over Sacramento again five days later, this time witnessed by thousands of people, including the city's deputy sheriff and a district attorney. Most agreed it was a cigar-shaped object of some size and that it moved slowly but methodically over the city before disappearing to the southwest. It supposedly appeared later that evening over San Francisco, some 90 miles away, where it was seen by hundreds of people and reportedly cruised over the Pacific Ocean, flashing its spotlight toward the Cliff House, one of San Francisco's most famous landmarks.

The area papers quickly caught "airship fever" and began reporting the mysterious vessel appearing elsewhere over California and as far north as Washington State and Canada. The sightings, however, abated by the end of December, and nothing more was seen of the mysterious "airship" for nearly two months. When it reappeared, it showed up far from California, this time over Hastings, Nebraska, on the evening of February 2, 1897. Soon it was spotted throughout the Midwest, from Texas to Iowa and from Kansas to Missouri. It even supposedly appeared over Chicago on the evening of April 11, where a photograph was reportedly taken (the first UFO photo on record, if authentic) and four days later over Kalamazoo, where it crashed and exploded, according to one local paper. Though reports continued after that, they soon diminished until by summer the airship flap of 1896–97 was over and the world was left with one more mystery to ponder.

Unanswered Questions

To this day, no one is certain what this object (or objects) might have been. Debunkers maintain it was all the product of yellow journalism—the tendency of newspapers to invent stories in an effort to increase sales—mixed with mass hysteria in which people imagined any light in the sky (sometimes speculated to having been an unusually bright Venus) to be the rogue airship. Today many in the UFO community, noting that UFOs are sometimes described as being cigar-shaped, have decided that these were early appearances by extraterrestrials, designed perhaps to test our level of sophistication (and apparently deciding we weren't ready for them yet.) Both explanations, however, leave us with more questions than answers.

The hoax/mass-hysteria theory, for example, fails to account for the initial sightings over California; newspapers didn't report on the object until after it had been seen by supposedly thousands of witnesses, while the mass hysteria theory fails to explain how such a thing can occur in a generally geographic straight line (moving from California through Nebraska and Iowa and finishing in Michigan.)

Even if we assume that the majority of reports were spurious or mistaken, it is curious how mass hysteria is capable of affecting only people along a particular path. Further, it is uncertain how many Midwesterners would have been aware of the earlier California sightings and so be inclined to imagine that the mysterious airship was headed their way; newspapers rarely picked up general-interest stories from other places in the country, preferring instead to stick with national headlines and stories of local interest.

Media coverage of the sightings tended to follow the appearances, not precede them as would be expected if the media were simply priming the country for more stories. Finally, the modern theory of extraterrestrials also seems unlikely, especially in view of the descriptions given by many witnesses that described propellers, wings, rudders, and undercarriages on the vessel—all appendages unlikely to be seen on an interplanetary vehicle.

So what was the thing that crossed the countryside that winter of 1896–97 to cause such a stir?

Interestingly, at the time most thought the vehicle neither imaginary nor extraterrestrial, but evidence of cutting-edge technology. They saw it as a very man-made machine being put through its paces by some intrepid inventor intent on bringing lighter-than-air flight to humanity. They thought it was a powered balloon or, more accurately, a dirigible.

Most dismiss this explanation, however, as being inconsistent with the capability of the time. The world was still in its technological infancy at this stage; although the lightbulb and the telephone had both been introduced, most people still used kerosene lamps and the U.S. mail to communicate. The Wright brothers were five years away from putting their tiny airplane into the air, and a practical automobile was still under development. The idea that anyone in that era could construct a working dirigible was beyond reason or, at least, so it seemed.

But can we really be so certain that the technology to build an airship was truly beyond the inventors of the late 19th century? A quick look into the history books will demonstrate how presumptuous this statement is.

Early History of Airships

Ever since the Montgolfier Brothers first flew their hot-air balloon over Paris in 1789, humans had been used to the idea of artificial flight.

What differentiated an airship from a mere balloon, however, was the ability to make it steerable, rather than being subject to the vagaries of air currents and wind. The first experiments to this effect were carried out by Britain's "father of aviation" Sir George Cayley in the 1830s. Unfortunately, Cayley lacked the means to effectively power such a ship and he gave up. Others, however, picked up on his ideas and further developed them until by 1850 a Frenchman, Pierre Jullien of Villejuif, demonstrated a model for a steerable airship. It was up to another Frenchman, Henri Giffard, however, to build and actually fly the first true airship in 1852. At 44 meters in length (almost 150 feet) and powered by a 2.2-kilowatt steam engine, he was able to travel the nearly 27 kilometers between Paris and Trappes, France, without incident, all at the remarkable speed of ten kilometers per hour.

Further development of the airship was made in the 1880s when Charles Renard and Arthur Krebs built an electric-powered model named La France that was able to maneuver under its own power. German designer David Schwarz built the first true dirigible (the earlier vehicles being essentially limp, cigar-shaped balloons tethered to a rigid undercarriage) and tested it at Tempelhof airfield in Berlin on November 3, 1897. Three short years later German general Ferdinand von Zeppelin would build his first airship, the LZ-1, and the age of LTA (lighter-than-air) travel was born.

Considering that airships had been under development in Europe prior to the airship flap of 1896–97, what are the chances that an American might have succeeded in creating the first practical and long-range example, the product of which would become the source of six months of sensationalism and rumor Let's consider the possibilities.

Overcoming the Technological Hurdle

The chief complaint made by many is that the materials and technology needed to construct a working airship were unavailable in 1896. We have already seen that such is not only untrue, but that proof of the concept had been demonstrated almost 50 years earlier. Connecting a series of hydrogen-filled balloons and enclosing them within a light but rigid frame of aluminum or wood was well within the capabilities of an 1896 inventor, given adequate resources and a building large enough to house the object. The problem would be finding a powerful enough engine to operate it. Diesel and gasoline-powered engines were still in their earliest stages of development in 1896, so it would have been difficult to make use of either of these two power sources. However, steam engines and electric motors were well known at the time (and, further, Giffard had demonstrated on his airship that a steam engine could be used successfully as a power source.) Other possible power plants include the electric motor, but this would have likely been hugely underpowered, requiring the use of several motors and a considerable number of heavy batteries to extend the range. But this might still be feasible if a person was able to find a way of combining an electric motor with kinetic energy; that is, several men pedaling a generator to charge the battery pack while in flight, thereby extending the range without having to carry too many batteries.

But what if we go beyond these traditional methods What if, in fact, we are dealing with someone who might be years ahead of the competition, both in terms of airship design and the power needed to run them? Rudolf Diesel had just introduced his revolutionary new power-plant just three years earlier; could someone have gotten hold of one of his early designs and improved upon it? There's also the chance that either the diesel or the gasoline engine could have been co-developed by more than one person at a time. Is it possible our mysterious inventor successfully developed his engine first and modified it for flight rather than for ground vehicles?

If this is what happened, why did this man not come forward with his invention for all to see? To answer this, we have to understand the mindset of the time.

The Need for Privacy

The last half of the 19th century was a time of remarkable technological advances and tremendous competition among inventors. It wasn't easy being an inventor in 19th-century America; the drive to be the first to the patent office was cutthroat in nature, with stolen ideas and even sabotage fairly common. They had to deal with pressure from investors eager to see a quick and handsome return on their money and, finally, they had the press (who could always be counted on to prematurely proclaim each new gadget a success or failure) to deal with. Considering that a single failure could easily scare away the capital needed to continue working, it is possible that a man would want to work in secret, away from the eyes of the media or potential competitors.

If that were the case with our mystery inventor, California would have been the perfect place to work. It was still remote enough to guarantee privacy and yet it was near enough to a major seaport and sources of capital to make it ideal. San Francisco had the largest number of millionaires of any city west of the Mississippi in 1897. It isn't difficult to imagine that a reclusive and possibly even eccentric inventor was able to not only find the required investment capital to build and operate an airship, but could construct the facilities necessary to maintain it (probably somewhere in the San Fernando Valley) in complete secrecy.

Of course, it would require considerable capital to make this work as well as a well-outfitted workshop (and the men needed to operate it), but would that be any more difficult to accomplish than it was for Bell or Edison, contemporaries of the era? The necessary equipment could easily be shipped from the East Coast to San Francisco, assembled in privacy, and be up and running in short order, all hidden from the general public and the media among the barren hills of Southern California.

The First Flights

The first sightings over Sacramento and San Francisco may have been early test flights of cutting-edge airship technology, a technology easily a decade or more ahead of its time.

Clearly, such is not an unreasonable hypothesis, considering that all the elements required to construct and operate a small dirigible (rubber air bags, girder material, steering gear, even various power sources) were all available by the mid-1890s. They awaited only a visionary with the brilliance, vision, and determination to bring it all together.

But if this mysterious inventor wished to work in secret, why fly over two of the largest cities in California and appear to thousands of witnesses, thereby announcing your presence? Simple: the design was nearing perfection and not only needed to be flown over long distances, making the avoidance of multiple witnesses difficult, but to send a message to the vessel's investor(s) that the ship was coming along quite nicely. Clearly, at some point the vessel was going to need to be unveiled to the general public; perhaps the sightings of November and December 1896 were just a sneak preview.

It's interesting that there was a two-month break between the California sightings in 1896 and the sightings in the Midwest in February through April 1897. This suggests that after initial test flights were completed, the inventor was ready to unveil his new airship by overflying America, the one way guaranteed to bring the most attention. By overflying the country, he was telegraphing his new device to the world in the most spectacular manner imaginable, perhaps with the goal of eventually landing on the East Coast in front of a stunned media.

But something happened that prevented him from completing that goal, something unexpected, sudden, and probably tragic.

A Fiery End or an Icy Grave

Newspapers reported an explosion in the night skies near Kalamazoo in April 1897, after which the airship sightings petered out and eventually ended. Could the still largely untested airship have exploded over Michigan or crashed into Lake Erie and sunk, abruptly and tragically ending its maiden flight?

Skeptics will point out that no wreckage was ever found. If it exploded (it was, after all, a hydrogen balloon) and fell into a dense forest somewhere in the Northeast, would there really be much left to recover? How much more so were it to have ended its flight in the frigid waters of Lake Erie?

The loss of the only airship and its brilliant inventor would have been irreplaceable; investors would have been unwilling to start from scratch and so they pulled the plug, and even the workshops would have been dismantled, the equipment and tools sold in an effort to recoup losses. Perhaps out of fear of ridicule or possible legal action, the inventor would have been quickly forgotten and the mysterious airship and its crew left to legend, where they could never be proven or disproven. It would have been a terrible tragedy, of course, and an incalculable loss to science, but such would have been the inevitable result of a noble but ill-fated experiment.

But what of the blueprints and engineering drawings such an undertaking would have produced? It is likely they were destroyed or otherwise lost. Perhaps one day they will be discovered and serve to tell the world that, just as the Antikythera computer (an analog device used to calculate the movements of stars and planets) demonstrated that technological genius existed 2,000 years ago, so too did we once have our own Archimedes of the skies under our very noses—or, in this case, over our very heads. We just failed to notice him until it was too late.

Aurora, Texas, and the Great Airship of 1897
By Kevin D. Randle

March 2003

Not long ago, I had the opportunity to appear on the late-night radio show, *Coast to Coast AM.* I bring this up only because, apparently, the next night the host had on Jim Marrs, who talked about the Aurora, Texas, airship crash of 1897. I wouldn't have known this, but someone who heard my interview the night before mentioned to me in an e-mail that Marrs had talked about Aurora and suggested that it was a real event. That person wanted to know if Marrs was correct and if there is anything to the story of the crash.

And this provides us with an opportunity to examine one of the major problems in UFO research. No case ever dies, no matter how many times it is exposed as a hoax. This is true even when those exposing it range from the skeptics to the believers in extraterrestrial contact. And it continues even when no evidence for the reality of the case has ever been found … or none was found until people began to realize they could get their names in the newspaper or their faces on television if they said something to confirm the case.

The stories of the flight of the Great Airship of 1897 provide us with proof of both theories. Although many of the tales have since been shown to be jokes, there are a few that are repeated in the UFO literature with such regularity, and almost with such awe, that it is necessary to provide, once again, all the information about them so that we can work to remove them from that same literature. The two most famous, and probably the most reported, are the Aurora, Texas, UFO crash that had been the subject of that e-mail correspondence and the Alexander Hamilton story of an airship and calf-napping that occurred about two days after the Aurora events.

Typical Airship Accounts

Back when I lived in Texas, I didn't live all that far from Aurora. I was interested in UFOs even then, and I prowled the morgues of various newspapers searching for stories of the great airship. There were lots of these stories from Texas, including interviews with the crews of some of the airships and even repeated tales of the airship's destruction.

Typical of the airship sightings was that told by Patrick Barnes to the Fort Worth Register, "which hardly cares to repeat it." He claimed that he was traveling near Cisco, Texas, and spotted several men standing around a large, cigar-shaped craft. He went over to talk to them and learned they were on their way to Cuba to bomb the Spanish. They had landed to make some repairs and soon took off. Their immediate destination was the Ozarks, where they planned to train for their self-designed mission.

In fact, there were dozens of stories of the Great Airship landing throughout the South and the Midwest in March and April of that year. One of the earliest appeared in the

Cedar Rapids (Iowa) Evening Gazette. According to the story, a large, cigar-shaped craft had landed on the Union Station in the "wee morning" hours and several locals were taken on board. Charley Jordan quickly made his story known to the newspaper and even signed an affidavit attesting to the reality of his flight. He was described by reporters as "never telling but a few lies and then only about things of importance."

He was accompanied by W. R. Boyd, whose whole purpose in going along, according to the newspaper story, was to "get as high as possible so that he could learn about the condition of the post office."

The airship's crew confessed that they were tired from their long journey, though they offered no revelations about their home base or their purpose. They did promise to lecture about the trip soon, and the topics to be discussed included the unlikely subject of hell.

The problem for Cedar Rapids was that, the very next night, the airship crashed in Waterloo, Iowa. Those in Cedar Rapids, who couldn't produce any physical evidence of their adventure, quietly faded from sight, while crowds flocked to the Waterloo fairgrounds, where they could see a large, twin-cigar-shaped object. A heavily accented "professor" claiming to be from San Francisco told of their perilous flight across the United States that ended in tragedy when their leader fell into and drowned in the Cedar River.

The whole story unraveled late in the day when the professor was recognized as a local man. The joke was admitted, and the "ship" was removed from the fairgrounds, but not before hundreds had the chance to see it and interview members of the crew.

The Aurora Crash

The Aurora crash story, as it was told just days later, suggests that the airship appeared about dawn on April 17, 1897, came in low, buzzed the town square, and then continued north toward the farm owned at the time by Judge J. S. Proctor. There it hit a windmill and exploded into a shower of debris, damaging the judge's flower garden and house, not to mention his windmill. The townspeople rushed to the scene and found the badly disfigured body of the pilot. T. J. Weems, a Signal Corps officer (the 1897 equivalent of an intelligence officer), thought the pilot was probably from Mars.

Being good Christians, and apparently because no one had anything else to do, they buried the pilot after a short memorial service that afternoon. They also gathered several documents covered with a strange writing found in the wreckage and picked up tons of material, including silver and aluminum that came from the airship. All that evidence has long since disappeared.

And that's it. No follow-up stories as tourists flocked to Aurora. No mysterious scientists arriving to inspect the wreckage. No Army response, though one of their own was on hand to report what he had seen. And finally, most importantly, no one ever produced those documents or bits and pieces of the wreckage, though there had been tons of it, at least according to the newspaper report.

The story died at that point, and then was resurrected in the 1960s by UFO researchers who stumbled onto the airship tales, which had been dormant for about six decades. Suddenly the story of the tragedy reappeared, and Aurora, Texas, was now on the map with those scientists, researchers, and tourists finally making the trek.

A large number of people, including Hayden Hewes of the now defunct International UFO Bureau; Jim Marrs, who had most recently suggested the story was real; and even Walt Andrus, the former International Director of the Mutual UFO Network (MUFON) at various times journeyed to Aurora in search of the truth. They all reported a strange grave marker in the Aurora cemetery. Using metal detectors, they found strange metal, and they gathered reports from longtime Aurora residents who remembered the story, remembered seeing the airship, or remembered parents talking about the crash. There was also discussion of government attempts to suppress the data. To them, that made the story of the crash real.

The problem here is that I beat most of these people to Aurora by several years to conduct my own investigation. I talked to some of those same longtime residents, who told me in the early 1970s that nothing had happened. I talked to the historians at the Wise County Historical Society (Aurora is in Wise County), who told me that it hadn't happened, though they wished it had. I learned that T. J. Weems, the famed Signal Corps officer, was, in fact, the local blacksmith. I learned that Judge Proctor didn't have a windmill, or rather that was what was said then. Now they suggest that he had two windmills. I wandered the graveyard, which isn't all that large (something just over 800 graves), and found no marker with strange symbols carved on it, though there are those who suggest a crude headstone with a rough airship on it had been there at the time. I found nothing to support the tale and went away believing, based on my own research and interviews, that this was another of the airship hoaxes.

Metal collected by all those others, when analyzed here, turned out to be nothing strange or unusual. Some of it was later analyzed in a Canadian lab, and their results mirrored those of American labs.

Isn't it interesting that none of the metal supposedly gathered by the town's residents has ever surfaced? The metal analyzed was always recovered by researchers with metal detectors. Isn't it interesting that the strange grave marker has since disappeared and that there is no real photographic record of it? There should be, for all the research that has been done. The single picture that has turned up showed not an airship but a coarse triangle with circles in the center. And isn't it interesting that there were never any follow-up reports from Aurora. First the big splash with the crash and then nothing for more than 60 years.

Another Fishy Story

Which also sums up nicely the Hamilton calf-napping story that followed the Aurora crash by two days. According to the literature, Alexander Hamilton was a widely respected resident of little LeRoy, Kansas. Jerry Clark reported that Hamilton had been a lawyer, had served in the Kansas legislature, and was a very successful stock dealer. Those who knew him suggested that he was an honest man.

According to the reports, including that in the Yate's Center (KS) Farmer's Advocate, Hamilton heard a disturbance among his cattle on Monday, April 19, and got out of bed to check. Hovering over his cow lot was the airship. It was, according to Hamilton, cigar-shaped, about 300 feet long, with some kind of a glass-encased carriage under it. Inside were six strange-looking beings who were at least human enough that Hamilton identified two men, a woman, and three children.

The craft hovered until the crew spotted Hamilton, his tenant Gid Heslip, and Hamilton's son. Then a great turbine wheel, about 30 feet in diameter, that had been revolving slowly below the craft, began to spin faster. As the airship climbed to 30 feet, it paused over a three-year-old heifer that was caught in a fence. Hamilton and his son found a cable from the airship wrapped around the cow and tried to free it from the cable, but couldn't. Instead, they cut the fence. The cow and ship began slowly rising and then disappeared in the distance.

The next day, Hamilton went in search of his missing cow but could find no trace of it. Instead, a neighbor, identified in the reports as Lank Thomas, had found the remains of a butchered cow several miles from the Hamilton spread. He picked up the remains and took them into LeRoy for identification. Thomas said he could not find any trace of a track in the soft ground around the cow's remains.

The newspaper, as well as other men in town, attested to the honesty of Hamilton, suggesting they all believed his ... well ... unbelievable tale. These men included an attorney, a doctor, a justice of the peace, a banker, and even the postmaster. If no other report from 1897 was to be believed, this one certainly had all the credibility that those others lacked.

And, like the Aurora crash, here was an 1897 report that seemed to mirror its modern counterparts. A UFO hovering over a ranch, an animal that disappeared and was later found mutilated with no sign of anyone being in the field with it. Unlike the modern reports, Hamilton saw the airship steal the animal rather than just vague, mystery lights glowing in the distance.

In the early 1970s, Jerry Clark managed to track down the relatives of Hamilton and interviewed an elderly woman, who remembered Hamilton returning from town, chuckling about the story he'd invented because it would be published in the newspaper. While that evidence might not convince a true believer, an article that appeared in the Atchison County (Mo.) Mail on May 7, 1897, should do it. Hamilton told the reporter, "I lied about it." Those who signed the affidavit about Hamilton's veracity were members of the local liars club.

What this tells us is that the newspapers, which had to suspect the truth if not know it outright, didn't mind printing the wildest tales of the airship. Proof of this comes from Burlington, Iowa, in what was described, even in 1897 as one of the "meanest and most discouraging [airship] stories of the entire lot." Members of the newspaper staff launched hot air balloons made from common tissue paper so that they would carry over the city. They soon began to receive reports from the citizens describing the airship. When one of the most distinguished men of that town came forward to report that he had not only seen the airship, but had heard voices from it, the newspaper staff was convinced that all the tales were faked. While their conclusion might seem premature at the time, later evidence would suggest that they weren't all that far off the mark.

Bull Market for Bull

Maybe part of it was the way many such stories were reported in 1897, especially those about the airship. The editors of the Cedar Rapids (Iowa) Gazette, upon learning the airship had landed in nearby Waterloo, wired their counterparts at the Waterloo Courier asking for 500 words but no crap. They didn't mention that their own story, carried a day earlier, was now clearly a hoax. They just ignored that fact. In other words, the newspapers were having some fun with the airship tales too.

In fact, that seems to cover the vast majority of the airship stories. The men telling them had ulterior motives for telling them. Maybe they just wanted to join the fun, or maybe they just wanted to see their names in the newspaper. Maybe they thought no one would be harmed, and, of course, no one was. Other news, more important news, finally pushed the tales of the airships from the newspapers and little was thought of them for decades.

The final, fatal blow for the airship and Aurora crash comes from the original reporter. H. E. Hayden, a stringer for the Dallas Morning News, claimed to have invented the story in a vain attempt to put his dying community back on the map. He hoped to draw attention, and people, to Aurora, Texas. He was successful. The problem was that he succeeded 60 years too late, and those who arrived only wanted to learn about the airship, not settle down to rebuild the community as he had hoped.

The Acknowledged Early Days

After the Kenneth Arnold incident, sightings multiplied astronomically, but no one really knew what they were looking at.

Now, 63 years later, people are still seeing things in the sky, but still no one really knows what they are looking at.

But it didn't take long in 1947 before a lot of people decided that the strange objects in the sky must be spaceships from another world. The late '40s witnessed a burgeoning of the phenomenon: the Roswell incident (virtually unreported and unknown at the time), the tragic Thomas Mantell crash, the Chiles-Whitted sighting from a commercial aircraft, the green fireballs in New Mexico, and countless others. It was also the era of the Air Force's feckless Projects Sign and Grudge, laying the foundation for the endless feud between the Air Force and UFO witnesses.

The 1950s were fun and scary at the same time. This is when all the classic, really interesting cases took place. You never knew what was going to happen.

Phantom Lights in Nevada
By Kenneth Arnold

Summer 1948

About every ten years, in the desert near the Oregon Canyon Ranch, which is located near McDermott, Nevada, mysterious lights are seen at night by sheepherders and cowboys. Although rarely receiving publicity, these lights are a frequent subject of comment and conjecture on the part of the local ranchers.

The elevation is approximately 4,400 feet above sea level, and the area is extremely dry. There is no swampland, no damp area that might account for the lights as "swamp-fire."

Sheepherders, most of them Basques (those strange people from the northeast provinces of Spain), have seen the lights most frequently, and describe them with complete and positive accord.

The lights, they say, appear somewhat like the lights of a car, but with either a pale red or a pale yellow gold, and hugging very close to the ground. The general appearance is as if someone was carrying a lantern, or a car was approaching. They are of a circular shape, glowing like a fluorescent light, and very often appear to be only twenty or thirty feet ahead of the observer. Yet, when approached, they seem just that much farther away. The lights have been chased as much as two or three miles, but never could the pursuer get close enough to determine the exact nature of the light. A series was seen in 1922, again in 1927, and others in 1930.

In 1930, Joe Bankafier, a rancher, was riding back to his ranch at night when he noticed a large, pale reddish glow or light, circular in shape, near the sheep corrals on his ranch at Oregon Canyon.

His horse carried him to within 50 yards of the light, then became frightened. Bankafier was unable to control the horse, which turned in terror, and ran with him for more than a mile. Finally exhausted, the horse pulled up, and Bankafier turned the animal around and tried to get it to return to the ranch. The horse went slowly, but remained nervous and jittery.

The light had disappeared, but when they reached the gate to the sheep corral, which was also the gate into the yard of the ranch, the horse refused to pass through the gate. Once more the horse bolted and ran with him a half-mile before he could bring it to a halt.

On the next try, he got off the horse and attempted to lead it through the gate. The horse refused to budge, became wild and panicky. Bankafier remounted the animal and once more tried to spur it through the gate. For the third time the horse bolted. This time, halting after a hundred yards, the horse turned, and proceeded to walk calmly through the gate, its terror completely vanished.

More than 50 of the sheepherders of the area have seen the mysterious lights, and it has been noted that dogs bark at them, proving they are visible to animals as well as humans.

The second type of mystery light seen in this area is best typified by the story of Tito Bengoa, one of three brothers who run the King's River Ranch near King's River, Nevada. Tito's brothers are Frank and Chris Bengoa, and all are Basques. The ranch usually runs 2,500 head of cattle, and its reputed to be worth a million dollars.

It was in 1930 that Tito Bengoa and his wife and a number of other persons went out into the desert and witnessed the phenomenon. They saw only one light, which seemed to travel along ahead of them, and at times, circle them. They could not tell what it was. It was rather disk-like or moon-like. It looked exactly like a full moon, but it was not the moon, evident by its travels around the party, and its passage between the party and the mountains in the distance.

The stories of Joe Bankafier and Tito Bengoa are confirmed by hundreds of residents of the valley and surrounding territory, and the reputation of each is unimpeachable.

What are the mystery lights of Nevada? To date there has been no satisfactory explanation.

The Mystery Ship
By L. Taylor Hansen

Winter 1949

No one doubts the reality of the mysterious spaceship seen over Alabama. But did it come form Mars

Of what origin is this "Mystery Ship?" Russian? That would be crediting them with an enormous engineering advantage over us. But if not, who then? Only two classes of persons would be willing to make the next guess-Mars. Those two classes might include astronomers (never for publication of course, only off the record), and science-fiction fans.

On the night that this story appeared in the newspapers, I looked up the authority on Mars—Lowell.

Percival Lowell established Lowell's Observatory in the highlands of Arizona during those years at the turn of the century when the western skies were still comparatively free of the soot and grime which churns them up today and which continues to pile an ever-mounting curtain of obscuring matter between our telescopes and the objects which they seek.

Every astronomer worthy of the name admits that Lowell had an advantage over them, even with his smaller telescope. In the rarest of fleeting seconds, or split seconds, when the obscuring film would clear, they too have seemed to catch a glimpse of the fine-penciled lines which astronomer Percival Lowell brazenly called "canals."

To Lowell, these waterways, which conducted the melting water from the polar caps down to and across the equator so that the deserts could flush green in the Martian springtime, could not be the work of chance. If they had been the work of chance, he argued, they would no climb from the swamps about the edge of the polar caps to the highlands of the deserts (comparative highlands since there are no mountains on Mars), nor would they cross the equator into the opposite hemisphere.

As he continued to view Mars, a still further conviction came to him. One can see it grow in his published works. These canals were turned off and on. One faded away and another came into view. He began to compute the time. One set was closed off for six Martian years (or twelve of our years) and another set turned on to service the same area.

But what did Lowell have to say about flying things- and lights After explaining that upon the moon the tops of its sharp peaks catch and hold the sunlight before the rest of the mountain is lighted, so that the peak seems to be a detached light on the rim for a time, Lowell continues on page 100 of *Mars and Its Canals*:

"Common upon the face of the Moon, excrescences of the terminator rim are rare on Mars. The first ever seen was detected by a visitor at the Lick Observatory in 1888.

Since then they have repeatedly been noticed both at Lick and elsewhere. But although observers are now on the watch for them, they are not very frequently chronicled because not of everyday occurrence. Much depends upon the opposition; some approaches of the planet proving more prolific of them than others."

Lowell continues to describe one such patch of light that could safely be relegated to the probability that it was a large dust storm, but his second description is more interesting.

"At the same time, Baltia, a region to the north of it and synchronously visible close upon the terminator, showed whitish. The seeing was good enough to disclose the Phison and Euphrates double (canal), the power of magnification of 310 and the aperture of the 24-inch objective.

"From the time it was first seen, the detached patch of light crept in toward the disk, the illuminated body of the planet. Four minutes after I first saw it, the dark space separating it from the nearest point of the terminator had sensibly lessened. So it continued, with some fluctuations intrinsic to the atmospheric difficulties of observations generally and to the smallness of the object itself, to become gradually less and less salient. It lasted for forty minutes from the moment it had first appeared to Mr. (V. M.) Slipher (astronomer at Flagstaff), and then passed from sight to leave the edge of the planet smooth and commonplace again."

The following day Lowell tells us that the entire staff eagerly watched to see if they could again see the projection. They did not see it was where expected, but a much smaller one was to be found farther north. It was so small in fact that only careful watching made it out or it would have been entirely missed. He then concludes by voicing one's own thoughts: Could these have been two different objects

Lowell is inclined to agree with W. H. Pickering, who considered these detached bits of moving light to be clouds. Undoubtedly some of them are. This view was strongly supported by fellow astronomer A. E. Douglass in a discussion about a large number of them that were observed in 1894 at Flagstaff. The mountain theory was shown to be untenable because of their movement.

Armed with these facts, I spent the next day actually looking up the men whose business it is to know Mars. I found them very cagey.

Yes, they had thought of Mars in connection with the Mystery Ship, but…but…

It was a possible explanation of course, but…but…

They were very shy about the use of their names. Off the record, well, that was another matter.

"If we could go along with Lowell and accept the fact that superior beings inhabited our neighboring planet, running thousands of miles of canal irrigation, they would naturally be disturbed by the atomic clouds whirled up from the Pacific Ocean in these past few months, which would undoubtedly show as great projections upon our terminator. If we could go along with Lowell, then these creatures of great engineering skill might decide that a cruise to Earth was in order to find out the reason for such projections. Perhaps they have been here thousands of times before and know all about us, even as we might watch a planet with an ant-civilization…with curiosity, but with no desire to communicate since no advantage could come to the more advanced group by such a communication."

These men of science even began to warm up to the subject and one suspected that some science-fiction talent might be hidden here.

"Perhaps all possible worlds are existing somewhere," one remarked. "Why not in a universe such as ours with its swarm of over a hundred million suns? Are we to believe the colossal egocentric proposal that we are the only fly-speck harboring life?"

"Or," proposed another, "how about the possible four hundred million other island-universes which we now think comprise our visible horizon"

"For a moment, gentlemen," I protested, "let us return to Mars. If such beings exist, why have they not tried to colonize Earth?"

I was pooh-poohed down immediately.

"What would make Earth desirable to a Martian? In the first place, do not forget the difference in surface pressure. Would you want to live your life in a suit of armor such as a Martian would have to wear to protect him from the intense pressure of our atmosphere compared to that in which he had evolved? You might want to go to the sea bottom to see what is down there, but ask any diver how long he wants to stay."

As I was about to return to my typewriter from the observatory in order to type this article, I thought of Dr. Robert N. Webster who once worked with the great tele-scope on Mt. Wilson, but who since has gone into another business and would probably not care if I used his name.

I told a thoughtful audience of observatory scientists how Webster, through one entire night had watched a tiny speck circle most of the Martian terminator, and on another occasion saw one cross the Mare Erythraeum (a region in the southern hemisphere of Mars that appears dark when viewed through a telescope) and continue down the lighter portion of the planet to the south. Webster had mentioned the fact that it was so small that he could not look right at it. He had to look away and then find it again later, which was not too hard, once he had discovered its direction of flight.

Then as I turned to go, it was the man who specializes on the study of the sun who gave me my parting thought.

"Has it occurred to you that if we could go along with Lowell, and grant a superior order of intelligence to the inhabitants of Mars, they would probably be rather worried by the manner in which our sun is acting lately? It is having a sort of fever—a rash of spots greater than have ever been observed before. Perhaps they have connected the atomic bomb bursts with these magnetic or atomic explosions upon the sun. The sun seems to react with a giant spot the day after a bomb is burst in the Pacific. After all, it is their sun too."

As I rode down the mountain, shielding the brilliance of our daystar from my eyes, his last words seemed to re-echo over and over in my mind...

"After all, it is their sun too..."

Space Ships, Flying Saucers and Clean Noses
By Ray Palmer

May, 1950

Let's assume that a space ship from another solar system landed at Aberdeen Proving Grounds...

Would the American people be told about it? Would it be attacked without warning, thereby violating the Constitution of the United States which provides that only Congress can declare war? Or would (providing intelligent contact was made with the crew of the space ship) a "secret" classification be placed on the whole matter, and at the discretion of high Army brass, would events be considered Army "property" and information received be used solely for Army purposes, and be withheld from any possible benefit for the Citizen? Would such information be turned (assuming it was technical knowledge greatly advanced over our own) to the purposes of armament rather than the purposes of peacetime technology? Would the American Citizen who wanted to know what was going on be told it was "none of his business?" Lastly, would he find himself "in trouble if he insisted it was his business? What kind of trouble? Would the advent of a space ship junk the American Constitution Just who is to decide just what the duty of the "guardians of National safety?" Has the average American anything to say about it?

First, let it be perfectly clear that, provided we are attacked by enemies from outer space, the U.S. Army has been hired to defend us. As tax-paying citizens of America, we shall require that the men whose salaries we pay for the purpose of shooting at invading space creatures, proceed with the shooting. Congress, hired for the purpose of declaring war when necessary, will back them up legally.

Today, all over the world, the military has "first crack" at any technological advancement. If it can be used for either offensive or defensive war, it is appropriated. If there is anything left over, it goes to the civilian, provided such use won't give the "enemy" any "vital" armament information.

Those who argue for preparedness have their point, and I won't dispute them. They fear Russia and perhaps with good reason. Apparently Russia fears us, and perhaps with equally good reason. Just a few moments thought on how much of my money is being spent for offensive weapons scares even me. I don't trust me at all. But that's the mental outlook of the whole world today, and it will take a great spiritual revival to change it—or a war which will leave us all flat broke and incapable of waging another, or even preparing for it. It's that mental outlook, which is one of psychotic suicidal tendencies, a mental disease, that is responsible for our army of "defense" which so interferes with our freedom, our privacy, our progress, our happiness, our peacefulness. Actually, we can't blame the brass for the polish we have given it by our stupid lack of interest in our welfare. We are too lazy and selfish to do our own work, and creating a peaceful world is hard work, so we let the hired help do it. Paradoxically, we hire warriors to make peace. How visitors from space must laugh at such stupidity, be amazed, and depart, shaking their heads.

What I am doing is "hitting back." When FATE first began its flying saucer investigations, it conducted itself in what it considered an absolutely fair way. It resorted to no "smear" tactics. It did not wax "sarcastic." It did not "belittle". It still refuses to resort to such tactics. But it will speak out in indignation, and defend itself. So, here it goes.

I wish to quote, first, a typical recent newspaper story quoting Army Intelligence. I will present it word for word, and then I will proceed to take it apart, as it deserves.

Army Tired of Reports
Flying Disks' Little Men Never There To Probers
Ya' seen any little 30-inch men around?
   From the phone calls and scattered reports, it would sound as if the Wellsian invasion of Men From Mars is at hand.
   At least three reports of these little guys landing in flying saucers have now been made. In one case, a bunch of them wearing gray uniforms and armed to the teeth spilled out of a flying disk.
   Where are they?
   When Army Intelligence officers investigate the possibility of an interplanetary invasion, the little men are not there.
   Tired after a two-year chase of 240 rumors (by actual count) of flying disks, Army Intelligence officers at Wright-Patterson Field, Dayton, OH, are refusing to "run down every silly story that comes along."
   However, Army Intelligence still classifies as secret a portion of its investigation.
   "It's nothing fearsome," an officer explained hastily.
   Previous to the report of six 30-inch men "burned and charred in a flying turtle disk" in the Sierra Madre Mountains in Mexico, Army Intelligence sifted a similar report in Wisconsin.
   A farmer said he watched a disk land.

> "Out of the saucer came a bunch of little men," he
> reported. "They were dressed in gray uniforms with
> red shoulder bars and wore red caps."
>
> Investigation revealed that the Wisconsin farmer
> has been discharged from the Army for mental reasons,
> Army Intelligence said.
>
> The probe was dropped right there.
>
> A popular magazine now publishes a report by two
> Death Valley prospectors of a 24-foot disk landing in
> the desert at a speed of 300 miles an hour.
>
> The prospectors, Buck Fitzgerald and Mace Garney,
> asserted they chased two 24-inch gents over a sand
> dune before losing them.
>
> Army Intelligence refused to swallow that one. Mag-
> azines such as this, it said, seldom have any evidence to
> support their fantasies.

There you have it. The "popular magazine" referred to is
FATE. The news story said it (FATE) "now publishes a report."
Actually FATE only repeated the report published by International News Service, and printed in hundreds of the
nation's newspapers. Therefore, the "suggestion," by infer-
ence, that FATE was the originator of the report, is a sample
of how attempts are made to mislead. Does the use of the
word "now" simply mean that Army Intelligence got "on the
ball" the minute they read FATE to attempt to discredit the
magazine? We think so. To sock it in solid, they add that
snide remark at the end of the article (which is certainly not
"news") that "magazines such as this seldom have any evidence to support their fantasies."

Right there is a sample of research, Army Intelligence
style. They label the story a "fantasy" without investigating.

How do they know it is a fantasy, if they do not investigate? Is it fair to judge without evidence? The Army says that's the way they judge. They admit it in part.

Well, maybe the Army dropped the Wisconsin investigation "right there," but FATE didn't. FATE went up there and discovered the following:

In and around the Waupaca area, Stevens Point, Wisconsin Rapids, dozens of reports were made, simultaneously by farmers and small-city folk, of "flying disks." All agreed that they were "tiny and brilliant" and flying both swiftly and slowly, and maneuvering in a way that eliminated the possibility of meteoric phenomenon. At least one person was injured by one. They either struck the ground and exploded violently, or exploded low over the ground. Fragments picked up looked like pieces of plaster of Paris. Fragments were remarkably few in number considering the apparent dimensions of the objects. All the reports FATE investigated were from honest, sane, hard-working farmers, at least one of them a very good friend of mine.

What these objects were, FATE has no theory to explain. All it knows is that they were seen, they maneuvered intelligently, they exploded, they left visible residue like plaster, they injured at least one person, they appeared in dozens of different localities in a hundred-mile area, and there were no little men, in uniforms or otherwise.

As for the Death Valley report, FATE covered that two issues ago. We pointed out there here, also, the Army seemed to go to great lengths to investigate in a particularly inept manner. Actually, we believe they investigated the matter thoroughly, and found it worthy of hushing up. But we don't believe they know any more than we learned from our Wisconsin investigation. In short, they are as baffled as we, but wouldn't admit it.

If the saucers were not founded on fact, why would they spend two years investigating the Sierra Madre turtle-disk affair and the charred corpses of the six 30-inch men, although it is very explicit about establishing he insanity of the Wisconsin farmer (whose name, by the way, is what?). If there were no charred corpses, they ought positively to state the fact. Now we're suspicious. We think there might possibly have been charred corpses, since it wasn't denied.

But of course, we are not to be given any information such as this. We citizens aren't supposed to be told, if there are spaceships from other worlds coming here, and actual other world beings' corpses found in their burned ship. We wonder why we can't be told. This is news.

We have already reproduced the non-secret portion of the official Project Saucer report made up by Wright-Patterson Army Intelligence officers. This non-secret report says the flying saucers are *real*. That there is a secret portion to the report leads us to believe that the information in it is even more sensational. Isn't it any of we taxpayers business? Are we in danger of being eaten by the nasty Martians, and not even being given the courtesy of providing our own salt?

"Ya' seen any little 30-inch men around?"

Whoever wrote that story ought to write for radio comedians—he's funny as a crutch.

And, since Army Intelligence won't report on the Mexico story, we will. Here it is: (the story is by Sam Petok, Free Press staff writer, who got his information secondhand from Alma Lawson, a Los Angeles businesswoman, who got it from a "sober and conservative scientist friend" whose name she refused to divulge. Pretty lousy evidence, but since Army Intelligence chose to mention the matter in showing how little evidence FATE has to support its fantasies, we'll have to present matter with as exact information as it is possible to secure.)

Interplanetary Saucers Discovered in Mexico

Those fascinating flying saucers that fired the imagination of Americans two summers ago have come south of the Rio Grande with an almost plausible twist.

It has been reported that dwarf men from another planet have penetrated the earth's atmosphere in a huge disk.

Two reports of silvery *platos voladores* as the disks are called in Mexico, were made almost simultaneously by commercial fliers about two weeks ago-one at Nogales, 60 miles south of Tucson, Ariz., and another at Tampico, 75 miles north of Mexico City on the Gulf of Mexico.

A third report was that a huge plato volador has made a soft landing on a mesa deep in the mountainous reaches of the Sierra Madre.

A native shepherd is said to have discovered the disk. Inside it, he reportedly found the charred and burned bodies of six men, all no taller than 30 inches.

Alma Lawson, a Los Angeles businesswoman, confided she had received this "authentic" information from a "sober and conservative" scientist friend whose name she refused to divulge.

She said he had been in the scientific expedition that visited the site about 15 days ago. Among the men were several physicists from the University of California, Miss Lawson said.

"The disk did not come from Russia," she declared. "All the information has been kept a closely guarded secret by both the American and Mexican Governments for fear of throwing the world into a turmoil."

Quizzed by the baffled but interested United States Embassy at Mexico City, the Mexican Ministry of Foreign Affairs dismissed the report as unfounded.

"We have no information on which to base any comment," it said.

At the outset a degree of credulity was given Miss Lawson's statement that both governments had ordered top-ranking American doctors and military men to the Capital, allegedly to examine the bodies.

Embassy officials, however, explained there was no secrecy involved in the congregation here of American Brass.

They are attending the Twelfth International Congress of Military Medicine and Pharmacy. Officials from 30 nations are meeting in Mexico City to set up an international code of military medicine.

The Lawson plato volador was a brownish metal, differing in color from the two disks reportedly seen by the pilots. About 100 feet in diameter, Miss Lawson said, the flying saucer was "so hard a hacksaw could not cut it."

She said her scientist friend had told her that the disk was shaped like a turtle and had a dirigible-like suspended cabin about 15 feet long.

Inside were the charred bodies of the midget men from another world, she said. One was sitting at the controls.

Miss Lawson said she had been informed that all six perished when the disk crashed into the earth's atmosphere, the friction setting them afire.

Automatic controls apparently guided the ship to a "soft and easy" landing.

The midget men bore all the physical and anatomical similarities to the human beings inhabiting the earth. Miss Lawson said she was informed by the scientist.

"This is 100 percent reliable," she insisted. "All of this information comes from an authentic source who is a very conservative man.

"I have been asked not to reveal his name because the investigation is continuing quietly from Washington," she said.

FATE has no faith in this story. The story, as it stands, is hearsay. If it is true, and it might be, we'll certainly get no information out of Army Intelligence and if said scientist were to come out and back Miss Lawson up, he'd be left high and dry with his "fantasy," simply because he couldn't show a "fried corpse" of a little man, or even a fragment of a *plato volador*. If he had a fragment, it would be termed "metallic rock found all through the Sierra Madre Mountains." Only, if you actually hunted for it, as at Tacoma, Washington, you'd find it singularly hard to find. All this, as the story by Miss Lawson states, "for fear of throwing the world into a turmoil."

Recently I was in New York City, where I met Stuart Rose, one of the editors of the Saturday Evening Post. I had arranged to meet with him on a story regarding another matter, and during the course of discussion, I resorted to a little trickery as follows:

"Mr. Rose, you ran one of my articles a few months ago."

"Is that so," said Mr. Rose.

"What article was that?"

"The flying saucer story, which you ran in two installments."

"Oh yes, peculiar thing, that was ... "

Here's where I resorted to a little trickery. Said I casually: "Yes, wasn't it I had a letter from the General the other day, admitting that the whole thing was inspired by the Army, and that the Post was only acceding to a request that the article be featured as a special favor."

Said Rose. "I still don't understand that whole affair. It was the craziest thing. I never did know what it was all about."

"Apparently it was an effort to reassure the American people regarding the flying saucers," I said.

"Many people are quite worried about them. And by the way, it certainly was not a very nice trick to play on the Post to announce, the very day the magazine appeared on the newsstands, that the flying saucers were "no joke."

Mr. Rose didn't say anything to that, but in his shoes I would have been very annoyed. It made a liar out of the Post.

"By the way," I went on. "I appreciate all the publicity the article gave to FATE. It helped our sale substantially.

Mr. Rose smiled wryly. "The Post never gives publicity like that," he said. "I can well understand your appreciation. But his was certainly unusual."

"I could really give you a flying saucer story," I remarked.

Mr. Rose could not have looked more disinterested.

In the light of this conversation, it would seem that little more need be said regarding the Post's saucer story. It was a fiasco that is typical of the lack of liaison between the branches of the Army. The Army inspires a story about how unreal the flying saucers are, while the Air Force at Wright-Patterson Airfield releases a story about how real they are. We prefer to agree with the Air Force.

Just to support that agreement, we'll present a few of the more recent flying disk reports.

Dave Johnson, aviation editor of the Idaho Statesman, went aloft with the deliberate intention of staying up until he saw a flying saucer. Here is his account:

"Three days of aerial search paid off Wednesday when for 45 seconds I watched a circular object dart about in front of a cloud bank. The object was round. It appeared black, although as it maneuvered in front of the clouds, I saw the sun flash from it once. I was flying at 14,000 feet west of Boise. I saw it clearly and distinctly. It was rising sharply and jerkily toward the top of the towering bank of clouds. At that moment it was round in shape. The object was turning so that it presented its edge to me. It then appeared as a straight black line. Then, with its edge still toward me, it shot straight up. When I landed, three men of the Idaho National Guard said they had seen an object performing similar maneuvers in the same area."

Dallas, Texas. A woman at Alvarado saw a bright, moon-like disk in the sky between 5 and 6 p.m. And, Mrs. Ramsey

C. Johnson, 929 South Oak Cliff Boulevard saw something large and white, going very fast.

Fort William, Ontario. Residents of Hymers, Ontario, saw a huge streak of fire race through the sky from the southwest. They saw it reached a point due west of Hymers, performed a loop, then moved south to disappear over the horizon.

Florida. W. R. Davis and P. L. Moore, Miami Weather Bureau, described an object somewhat smaller than a full moon. It lit up the sky to the northwest and fell vertically, leaving a luminous, weaving trail. The trail was S shaped. The object was also sighted at Cedar Keys, with a tail estimated 50 to 60 miles long. The phenomenon was seen as far north as Brunswick, Georgia.

Salem, Oregon. A dozen persons reported that while they were watching the maneuvers of a number of airplanes they observed a flying saucer en route north. After proceeding north for some distance, it turned around and headed south. It halted twice after making the turn. The observations were made from Fairmount Hill, one of the outstanding residential sections.

Seattle, Washington. Three mountain climbers were buzzed by a flying saucer that was round, almost transparent and sounded like a buzz saw. Roger Hamilton, his wife, Patricia, and Dick Hamilton said they sighted the object near Snow Lake on the Snoqualmie Pass. It went so fast none of them had time to take a picture.

John J. O'Neill, NHYT News Service, had his telescope pointed at the moon, when a dark body moved across its face from east to west in about one and one half seconds.

It was approximately oval, with an angular dimension of between six and ten seconds of arc, was in sharp focus, and cut in a straight, sharply defined path. It was small, but could have been seen by the naked eye. It was obviously a celestial object and not a night-flying bird, dark airplane, or other such terrestrial object. It was obviously moving in space between in space between the earth and the moon. If a satellite of Luna, the high velocity with which it was moving would require that it be very close to the moon. If its distance was only 4,000 miles from the Earth, it would be moving with a velocity of 12 miles per second, and would be about 500 feet in diameter.

Louella O. Parsons, famous movie columnist, reported the fantastic story of 900 feet taken of the flying saucers in Alaska.

Over a year ago, *Mikel Conrad* was in Alaska filming *Arctic Manhunt* when he heard from the Eskimos of strange flying disks. He made a trip into the Frozen North to see for himself. Then he reported to Washington. The government sent a man to Alaska and asked Conrad for the film he had taken. He turned it over to them. After examination, it was placed in a sealed vault in Los Angeles. Now the film has been released to Conrad, who is incorporating it into a film called "*Flying Saucer.*" Howard Irving Young is writing the film. Conrad is a producer and director for Colonial Pictures.

Boston. Farmer Joseph E. Panek, of South Sedick Road doesn't believe a thing unless he sees it. He, his wife Clara, and a neighbor, Michael P. Bednasz were putting corn in a silo. Panek looked up and saw an object, round like a ball or a saucer, traveling very fast, maybe 1,000 miles per hour, from west to east. It was light and silvery looking and left no smoke or noise. Both his wife and neighbor saw it when he shouted.

Milford, Ohio. 6,000 to 7,000 saw a flying saucer during the St. Gertrude festival at Madeira. Sgt. Berger, operating a searchlight owned by the St. Peter and Paul Church at Norwood caught the disk in his beam. The saucer immediately moved up and out of sight. Berger caught it again two hours later, and this time it did not try to move up. It was under continuous observation for two and one half hours more. Berger estimates it was at an elevation of seven or eight miles. It was apparently 100 to 150 feet in diameter. It seemed to be made of aluminum or some shiny material. The longer the light remained on the disk, the greater the intensity of its glow became. Berger experimented- he moved the light, and the disk remained visible, glowing brightly. Then it moved back into the beam of its own accord.

A Milford family drove over, informed Berger that from their viewpoint the disk seemed to be two globes, one above the other. Looking straight up, reported Berger, was like looking at the bottom of a plate.

Temagami, Ontario. A jagged, sustained flash of blinding light that lasted for several minutes was seen moving between Timmins and Temagami. It was a tremendous bluish-white flash, and the illumination remained in the heavens for between six and seven minutes. It was not the aurora borealis.

Osborne, Kansas. Delmar Remick looked up when he heard geese honking. He saw a flying saucer in the air about a mile up, heading northwest. It remained in view six or seven seconds, moved at terrific speed. Its only other motion was a sort of little flip about every half-second.

There are hundreds more such reports, from every area. They cannot be denied. There is something going on in the sky that is beyond the knowledge of our scientists. The fact remains, there are "flying saucers" and they perform with incredible ability.

In the introduction to this article, we asked what would happen to a citizen who tried to learn something about the mythical space ship that landed at Aberdeen Proving Grounds, insisting that it was his business too. We inferred he might be in trouble, and we asked what kind of trouble.

Well, we have an answer to that which is based on experience. No, we haven't seen a space ship at Aberdeen Proving Grounds, but we know what kind of trouble John Q. Citizen can get into if he happens to turn onto a road labeled "Brass." Telling you about it will give you some idea of what really would happen if that spaceship landed, and was classified by the army. "Classified' means "none of your darn business."

Easter Sunday, 1941, several conditions existed which are important: 1. The United States was not at war. 2. Canada was. December 7th was still three quarters of a year away.

On that Sunday, the writer drove from Chicago to Sault Ste. Marie. With him went a young girl whose husband-to-be was stationed with the armed forces at the famous locks.

She wanted to see the young man. It was as simple as all that.

As often happens in that North Country, it snowed. Huge drifts made it impossible to drive back. So, leaving both the young girl and the car there, we returned to our job in Chicago.

A month later, opportunity came to return and retrieve the car, and we hoped, attend a wedding. As it turned out, there was no wedding, and we set out to return to Chicago from the Canadian side of the river.

At the ferry an immigrations official motioned us to park the car. "Routine check," he said briefly.

It was far from routine. We were separated, and questioned. After some six hours I finally reached the decision that something was decidedly wrong about the setup. I requested to be conveyed to the American authorities. Since I had paid my ten cents on the ferry, declared my name and status as an American citizen, and thus entered Canada legally, I requested to return the same way.

After several hours wait, American army officers arrived. I was driven across in an army car, my own car nowhere visible. I did not see it again for a week. When I did, I found that it had literally been taken apart. I am sure not even the battery cells were overlooked in one of the most systematic searches I have ever seen.

Briefly, the Colonel summed it up for me.

"You are," he said, "the cleverest spy we have ever run across."

"Spy!" I gasped. "Clever"

"Yes," he said. "For one whole month we've had dozens of our best men trailing that car, and were unable to discover how contacts were made between the girl and the mastermind."

"The mastermind"

"Yes! You. Anybody who could evade our search of the area for that length of time is supremely clever."

"I am flattered—but confused," I confessed. "Perhaps the reason you couldn't find me here was because I was in Chicago. And just what is it I am supposed to be masterminding?"

"Perhaps I had better refresh your memory," he said. "First, in searching your baggage, we found the photo you took of the airport in that yellow plane Saturday morning."

"Photo—yellow plane?"

"Yes. Yesterday morning you flew over the area in an unmarked plane. We shot at you, but missed. We haven't found the plane yet, but now that we have you, it'll only be a matter of time."

"I wish I could help you," I offered. "But go on. I am beginning to get interested in this little joke. I have some friends in the army, but I didn't know any of them were stationed here."

"This is no joke," he assured me. "But to get on, a month ago you..." His voice trailed off and he turned and produced a wooden box with a hold drilled in one side of it about an inch in diameter. Mounted in the hole was a piece of glass that certainly was not a lens. Inside the box were several dry-cell batteries hooked up in series. There was nothing else.

"What is it?" asked the Colonel.

"I give up," I said helplessly. "It looks like a doorbell."

"Don't try to be funny," he said dangerously. "You'll make it a lot easier for yourself if you confess."

"What is it you want me to confess?"

"All right, if that's the way you want it. A month ago you used this death ray to shoot down six of our barrage balloons."

"I did?" I faltered weakly.

"Yes. And the same night you instigated a riot on the Canadian side, which resulted in a pitched battle between United States artillerymen and Canadian troops. In that battle a house was burned down, a man burned to death, and a small child suffered a broken leg and exposure, which resulted in pneumonia and death. You have been positively identified as being on the scene. Do you deny it?"

"I don't deny being there," I admitted. "But my amazing participation I cannot remember. As I remember it, that night a storm started, an electric storm, which later developed into a snowstorm that stopped all auto traffic. During the electrical storm, several barrage balloons were struck by lightning. One of them fell on a house on the Canadian side. It burned. Because it was an American barrage balloon, Canadian troops surrounded the house to prevent any altering of evidence, or something of the sort. Several American Negro soldiers, insisting they saw a face at the window, attempted to rescue the inmates. A battle resulted. It turned out that a man was burned in the fire, and a little girl jumped out of the window, suffered a broken leg, and because it was cold and wet, obviously contracted the pneumonia you mention. But the rest of it sounds absolutely fantastic to me."

"You threw this death ray into the river," he accused, "but didn't throw it far enough. It landed on the bank, in the weeds, and we found it."

I looked at the box. "If that is a death ray," I said, "I am an Eskimo."

At that moment a lieutenant entered the room, whispered in the Colonel's ear. He turned to me triumphantly.

"We've caught your confederate," he announced.

"Amazing," I said. "Who is he?"

"The operator of the steam shovel in the new lock. He has just sabotaged the whole thing for months, but uprooting the adjoining lock and flooding the whole workings. We've got you now!"

Then began a grilling that made the rest of it seem like child's play. To me, only one incident stands out as important. I had written eight single-spaced typewritten pages of my impressions of the relations between Canadians and Americans at the Sault, and I now realized that it in the light of all these other fantastic accusations, the statements therein would be construed at the very least as seditious. I had these sheets in a legal-sized envelope. Two men, a Captain and a Lieutenant searched me. I emptied every pocket at their instructions, transferring this tremendously large and noisy envelope from pocket to pocket, just on the hope that they might not see me do it. It was impossible—but like everything else that happened on that crazy trip, the impossible happened—they seemed to be as blind as bats. Later I tore up the sheets and flushed them down the toilet.

During the week that followed (it took that long, they said, to develop the negative of the airfield and discover that it really was a picture of Hiawatha Falls, as I had claimed, and the runways were really a cable fence protecting persons from falling into it). I despaired of ever seeing Chicago again.

When I demanded to know what were the charges against me, the Major told me any charges I wanted. He suggested a few. "The Mann Act, for instance. I have several soldiers who will confirm the immortal purposes for which you transported Miss _____ across the Michigan State line..."

"Skip it," I said hastily. "But I want to see a lawyer."

"I'm a lawyer," he said. "And a good one."

"At least let me call my boss and tell him why I'm not at my desk."

"Don't worry about it."

In short, I insisted on my Constitutional rights, found I had none. I was held incommunicado. I was not allowed to see a lawyer. I was treated, in at least one instance, violently, although I must admit it was a Canadian who did it, and who came off second best—my nose didn't bleed.

All because Army Intelligence was looking for a mystery yellow plane which had ignored a challenge in flying over the area; because lightning had obviously struck a series of barrage balloons; because a small boy's attempt at a "gadget" had been found beside the river; because your "mastermind spy" was editor of a science-fiction magazine, and therefore knew all about death rays—and just happened to be there!

Funny. Yes, it was. But my rights as a citizen were violated, and although it is true that I could have raised a stink about it later, the stink would have gotten exactly nowhere.

More than $50,000 of taxpayers' money was spent flying my fingerprints to Washington, flying Army Intelligence men to every member of my family, every acquaintance, every business associate, in absolutely fantastic investigation. I suffered extreme loss of reputation, incurred the suspicion of numerous persons, lost important and valuable business contacts, lost financially, and got pushed around. And the funniest line of the whole comic opera was the parting shot of the Colonel, who had turned America upside down to find just one thing against my record to justify having me (I felt almost sure) shot on the spot (which could have been done, by the simple expedient of shipping me back to Canada where my "crimes" had occurred).

Said the Colonel: "We've found that you have a clean record, but if you'll take my advice for the future, keep your nose clean!"

I can think of only one way to do it successfully, where the Brass is concerned—go to bed and stay there!

I've often wished that Colonel would come to my office looking for a job—I've prepared an application blank that is a lulu. Come sneaking into my office, secretly plot to take over my job, and blow up my printing presses, will he!

Recently, Professor George Adamski of Palomar Gardens gave a speech before the Rotary Club of Fallbrook, California. According to Professor Adamski, the flying saucers seen by many at various times during the past few years are huge space ships from some planet, probably Mars!

"Ghost ships were discovered and pronounced real two years ago," said Professor Adamski. "Saucers, seen by thousands, are not flights of fancy, but ships from planets. These ships have been seen by radar on the other side of the moon. They are better than 700 feet long. They have approached as close as 30 to 40 miles above the earth, flying at speeds of 2 to 3 miles per second.

"These space ships will land here soon, from which planets we do not know, but science now claims that all planets are inhabited.

"Photos of Mars taken from Mt. Palomar have proven the canals on Mars are man-made, built by an intelligence far greater than any man's on earth.

"Science and the Navy know that we can land a ship of 40 men on the moon; and the next war we will require another planet to fight from. In line with this endeavor, Westinghouse is now building a cosmic ray motor run by light.

"Science is now working on a combination of radar and television that promises within two years the home-set will get space pictures at any distance."

According to Professor Adamski, the saucers merely appeared to be close to the earth. Their passengers were evidently merely getting a close-up look-see of our puny efforts of doing-over the world, but hesitated to come too close or land for fear of our anti-craft guns.

He placed America in the kindergarten, scientifically and intellectually, while the supermen from Mars, Jupiter and a billion satellites will soon be dropping on our acres.

But he kicked the Orson Welles theory out of the window. Mars-men will be friendly. In fact, so different from

Americans that the Navy has started an intensive training of crewmen in courtesy. This group will also be the first to be sent to the moon.

Professor Adamski points out that the news is already obsolete. All knowledge of space ships is a military secret until such time as new knowledge supplants it. What is told the public is no longer important.

There is no reason to believe that of the millions and possibly billions of stars and planets floating in endless space, our earth should be the only one that is inhabited and that our intelligence exceeds that of any of the others.

We do know that the atmosphere of Mars contains much less oxygen than the atmosphere of the earth. In fact the air is so rarefied that an oxygen-filled human from this earth would probably blow up if he stepped out of a pressurized cabin of a space ship to the soil of Mars, and by the same token, the body of Marsman would probably collapse if he emerged from his space ship when he reached the earth.

Professor Adamski's book, *Pioneers of Space* will be off the press in two weeks. The Navy has already ordered 50.

FATE reads this account of Professor Adamski's speech with skepticism. It strikes us as being filled with romance and quite a bit of hot air; yet it mentions several things we wonder about, namely those radar observations of space ships on the other side of the moon, meaning, no doubt, beyond its orbit, not on its other side, which never faces the earth. An object 700 feet long at that distance would be quite some gnat in the Polo Grounds (home of the Brooklyn Dodgers). And the observation by Palomar of the Martian canals, and positive identification as canals. We haven't had that confirmed; rather, it has been denied. Westinghouse is certainly building something, if it is building such a motor as is described. We'd like to see it.

We'd like to read his book. We hope it makes more sense than his speech. But we have given it to you for what it is worth.

Now, finally, we have gotten the complete report given by Captain C. S. Chiles and copilot John Whitted, of Eastern Airlines concerning the "space ship" they saw. On Saturday morning, July 24, 1948, at 2:45 a.m. they were flying at about 5,000 feet and were watching faint flashes of lightning ahead of them ...

We had our eyes focused on the point from which the thing came. From the right and slightly above us came a bright glow and the long, rocketlike ship quickly took form in the distance.

"It's a jet job," I said to Whitted, my copilot.

Then it grew larger and pulled up alongside. It appeared to be about 100 feet long, with a huge fuselage, probably three times as large as that of a B–29.

"It's too big for a jet, but what the devil is it?" said Whitted.

There were two rows of windows and it appeared definitely to be a two-decker. The lights from the inside were a ghastly white, like the glow of a gas light—the whitest we'd ever seen.

There was a long shaft on the ship's nose that looked like it might have been part of the radar controls. The ship acted that way, too, for just after it pulled alongside us, it whipped quickly upward at a very sharp angle. It certainly was maneuverable, because it made that turn fast as lightning. It disappeared into the clouds and reappeared again for several times before we lost sight of it.

There appeared to be windshields from two or three of the front windows. Whether those apertures were all windows, or whether some of them were breathers to feed oxygen to a fire inside, we don't know. The more we think about the white glare, the fluorescent glow underneath and the cherry-red flame it belched behind, the more we're convinced it was a rocket ship.

John Whitted piloted a heavy bomber with the 20th Air Force during the war and I served in all theaters with the Air Transport Command, so we've seen about every kind of known aircraft. This monster was like nothing we'd seen before. It was too close to us, and too clear in detail to be anything but a man-made ship.

We've considered, of course, the remote possibility that it was a ship from another planet. We prefer to believe that it's one of our own ships that's still a military secret. I'd certainly hate to know that our air force would have to face a fleet of machines like that.

We were both stunned, and didn't say anything for several minutes. It was so awe-inspiring that it just paralyzed us for the moment.

Then I said to John, "Am I crazy?"

"I'm crazy, too," he said.

"I'm going back and see what the passengers saw, if you'll take over," I told John, and I rushed back to the passengers.

They were all asleep but one. He asked me what it was that just passed us, said it went by so fast he couldn't make it out. He said he was too startled to note details. He is C. L. McKelvie, an amateur photographer of Columbus, Ohio.

McKelvie had a camera on a strap around his neck. He said he didn't have time to snap a picture. It occurred to me that I also had a camera with me. I was too busy looking at it to think of the camera.

Lots of persons think we're kidding, but the more we think about it the more serious we are about it...

FATE gives you the complete and unvarnished story here. Any other version is untrue.

Now, let's summarize what is actually known of the flying saucers. We'll merely list the facts without embellishments, and when we have finished, challenge anyone to say there aren't flying saucers.

1. Although many people saw these strange objects in the sky previous to Kenneth Arnold's now-famous report, his was the first story to plunge them into the limelight. Altogether he has seen them three times, and on two occasions obtained photos, which lack details, but which show that something was there.

2. Thousands of persons of unimpeachable integrity have confirmed his observation.

3. Dozens of photos have been taken of flying saucers, including a very good one at Phoenix, Arizona, one at Seattle, another at Toronto, one by the Army over Nova Scotia, 900 feet of movie film in Alaska, one in Los Angeles, and one at Morristown, New Jersey.

4. Space ships or flying saucers have been tracked by radar in hundreds of instances, but most notably at White Sands Proving Ground, where they followed experimental V-2 Rockets up to 104 miles and down again at speeds of 4 miles per second.

5. Army pilots have chased them repeatedly—one National Guard pilot being killed in such a chase, on a sighting later declared to be something other than the explanation that it was the Planet Venus, as was first suggested. Scientific evidence disproved that claim. Another pilot over Fargo, North Dakota, fought a weird flying duel with a strange glowing disk that went one for half an hour and was witnessed by many.

6. Fragments of a flying saucer (claimed by Air Force Intelligence to be metallic rock common on the West Coast) which reportedly was in trouble over Maury Island, Washington, revealed under analysis they were not rock, but man-made, and containing unaccountable amounts of calcium which did not vaporize at 2,500 degrees, and titanium, the metal being considered as the only one suitable to spaceships, in unusual combination. In this case, the Air Force claimed the participants had confessed it was a hoax, yet FATE received a vigorous denial of this, labeling it "a bold-faced lie."

7. A special investigating team was set up called Project Saucer, which investigates all reports of flying saucers, 40 percent of which cannot be explained away. (Latest report is that Project Saucer was abandoned in September, 1949.)

8. As much pressure as possible was and is being brought to bear to suppress, discredit and disprove reports of flying saucers or space ships.

9. Officers of Project Saucer prepared an official statement which declared the flying saucers are real, that they do not come from our solar system, but from one of 22, the nearest of which is eight light years away (Light travels 186,000 miles per second.)

10. A story belittling the flying saucers was placed in the Saturday Evening Post.

11. Project Saucers investigated FATE's editor repeatedly, using various disguises, sending official representatives, including members of other branches of the secret service such as the FBI, Central Intelligence, and we even received a visit from the famous Baron X. Baron Eduard Graf von Rothkirch of Hillman, Minnesota, was head of a famed spy group, the Frie corps of Barbarossa, the only group able to penetrate the Soviet Iron Curtain (so he said, and so Drew Pearson said, which doesn't mean much).

12. There are four distinct types of flying objects: the saucer (or disk), the crescent, the rocket-ship type, and the giant golden (or orange sphere).

13. Radar detections of mysterious objects are common, even showing solid objects where nothing is visible at all.

14. Today's reports are similar to reports gathered by Charles Fort, covering events of more than two hundred years.

15. Hundreds of reports, following a definite and recognizable pattern, which prove their authenticity, come in every month from all over the United States, and from other portions of the world.

16. The aerodynamic principles of the flying disk are admitted by the Air Force, and it is quite probable that secret work along these lines may be going on, accounting for some of the sightings of non-spectacular nature. However, the performance of many of these objects precludes our own mechanical ability being responsible, and makes operation by humans such as we impossible.

17. Many hoaxes have been penetrated, ranging from hot stove lids to furnace tops fitted with rocket tubes and fake radio gadgets, and flying circular saws hurled from church towers. Among such hoaxes is the photo of a flying disk settling into the Wolf River in Canada, reported in FATE Summer edition, 1948. This was a hoax engineered by science-fiction fans, and was achieved by exploding something beneath the surface of the water, and photographing it at the instant of detonation.

18. A B–25 from Hamilton field crashed at Kelso, Washington, carrying a large box of fragments, which were found in the wreckage. For some reason, their presence was denied.

19. The pilot of the B–25 was a member of Central Intelligence, the highest branch of the Secret Service in the United States, answerable to no one except extremely

high officials establishing the importance of flying saucer investigation.

20. Flying saucers travel far faster than the speed of sound with great ease, and in no instance has one of our planes been able to catch or keep up with one. Nor can any of our planes travel to the heights to which Saucers have been seen to go.

21. We don't know what the flying saucers are.

As for Army Intelligence, we suggest they read *Buck Rogers* with great care, and then at least they'll know as much about space ships as the average American Boy. And if they're keeping anything from his tender mind, don't bother! He's the lad who's going to Mars, when Americans go there, not the "guys" who write this "inspired" poppycock we see in newspapers and magazines these days. Writers such as these seldom have any evidence to support their fantasies.

Phantom Lights in Oklahoma
By William Bathlot

January 1952

A little story by Kenneth Arnold entitled "Phantom Lights in Nevada" came out in fall 1948, FATE magazine. (Also see "Lights Without Flame." August-September FATE.) I wish to verify Mr. Arnold's story with one of my own and, at the same time, to point out that these mysterious lights are not confined to Nevada alone. To my certain knowledge we had these same lights away back before 1900 and since in the Texas and Oklahoma Panhandles and also in the lower parts of Kansas.

About 1900 the government opened up the land in Beaver County in the Oklahoma Panhandle to homesteaders. At that time the entire country was covered with bunch grass and blue stem and pastured by thousands of head of cattle from ranches up and down the Cimarron and Beaver rivers. I filed on a relinquishment in the year 1905, built a dugout and a little one-room shack above it.

A cowpuncher friend of mine from the (X–I) Ranch, over on the Cimarron river, and I were sitting out in front of my shack one warm June night when a light about the size of a boy's toy balloon suddenly appeared 100 yards west of the house and moved leisurely along toward the north. It seemed to float about a foot and a half above the ground and threw out a yellowing glow.

"Jim," I asked, "Who do you suppose is tramping across the country with a lantern at this time of night?"

"Just a ghost light," Jim explained, as casually as if he slept with them. "From what I can find out, this country has always been pestered with them. They're spooky all right. Can't get a cow pony near one. Nothing slower than lightning can catch up to them. They can turn off and on whenever it suits them. No one knows what they are. But since they don't do any damage, we pay them no mind. Speaking for myself, I can't lose any of them and, furthermore, I don't intend to get too friendly with the critters!"

But I have the same curiosity that killed the cat and I decided to meet the ghost the first chance I got. I did some figuring. This wasn't a will-o'-the-wisp or a jack-o'-lantern type of infestation of low, swampy land. The dry upland of the Oklahoma Panhandle doesn't breed those and, besides, these lights were too large and not the color of swamp lights. Since we have electric eels, luminous fish, and fireflies, I thought, it is reasonable to believe that large birds of some unknown species live on the western prairies and are able to illuminate their bodies.

Several times that summer I saw strange lights at a distance, but I never was able to get anywhere near one. Then, one night as I was coming home from Liberal, Kansas, with a load of lumber, a luminous globe of light, somewhat larger than a man's head, sprang into sight on the road about ten feet ahead of the team. The horses, badly frightened, jumped sideways, crowding a front wheel beneath the wagon and nearly upsetting the load of lumber.

This ball of light seemed to throw out a dim glow, but it gave forth no rays. It kept to the road ahead of the team. As I came down a slight incline I put the team into a fast trot thinking I might get close enough to the light to see what it was. And I did get close enough to see the outlines of the road right through it. Then, as if fearing capture, it rose into the air and settled a short distance from the road.

I pulled the team to a halt and walked over to a patch of wild plum brush where I thought the object had come to rest, but I couldn't find a thing or hear a sound, thought I felt some sinister thing was watching my every move and cold chills ran up my back. In spite of all this, I remained convinced that I was on the trail of a large luminous bird.

A month after this old Brindle, the cow, about to come in fresh, struck out one evening for the timber along the Cimarron River two miles away to the north. Bob, my saddle pony, had cut himself across the chest on a barbwire fence the day before so I had to take out after old Brindle on foot.

The country was as dry as a powder horn that fall, and the coyotes seemed more numerous than usual. I picked up my double-barreled shotgun, slipped some loaded shells into my pocket, took my hired hand, and started over the trail to find the cow.

It was dark when we found her. Brindle had found her calf and she didn't intend to go back home with us. We couldn't very well carry the calf, so we decided to return early in the morning with the team and wagon, load the calf in the wagon and lead the cow.

We were a mile from home when, without the slightest sound, a ball of luminous fire appeared just ahead of us in the trail. We stopped in our tracks and watched it in silence for a while. We tried walking around it but it would slide over and head us off. When we went forward it backed up and when we backed up it came toward us.

We just stood there with that thing about a dozen feet in front of us as silent as death itself. It was transparent. We could see a bunch of sagebrush right through its body. It hovered in the air approximately 18 inches above the ground. We could see no body resembling bird or animal, nor could we see anything resembling legs to hold it up. It was just a ball of light.

Yet apparently this strange object could see us, and it checked our every move. The deadly unnerving stillness of the thing seemed to paralyze us. Finally I raised the shotgun to my shoulder and let it have both barrels. The light went out.

We didn't stop to see what, if anything, we had hit but hurried on home. The next morning, when we went after the cow and calf, we stopped the team near the spot to see what damage we had done. We examined the place carefully.

There was no blood, no feathers, no hair, and no footsteps except our own in the fine blow sand that covered the earth.

I went back to Forgan, Oklahoma, on a visit a year ago. That night, far in the distance to the southwest, we saw two of the ghost lights. These were not car lights, for cars do not travel deep Oklahoma blow sand where there are no roads. Sometimes I wonder if these ghostly lights are the spirits of men who died in old No Man's Land when Judge Colt ruled the Oklahoma Panhandle with his six-gun!

TWO: Roswell

Among the most spectacular cases of the late '40s was the alleged UFO crash near Roswell, New Mexico, on July 2, 1947, only eight days after the Kenneth Arnold sighting 1,600 miles away. Very little was made of the incident on the national level until investigators, notably Charles Berlitz and Stanton Friedman, began looking into the case many years later. Since then, the Air Force has come up with four distinct and mutually exclusive explanations of what actually happened, and none are satisfactory. It is certain that something did crash, but whether it was a Mogul balloon or an extraterrestrial spacecraft with alien bodies aboard seems open to endless speculation and conflicting reports from a variety of ex post facto witnesses—many of them now dead, others approaching senility, and all of several degrees of reliability. Very unsatisfactory, especially since whatever hard evidence there might have been has vanished into official vaults. Despite the difficulties of investigation, however,

Roswell has become the best known of all saucer cases and goes far toward supporting the local economy. But it offers the most obvious and undeniable instance of the frequently alleged government cover-up of anything relating to UFOs. They are certainly covering up something, but what?

Roswell Finale
By Stanton T. Friedman and John A. Keel

September 1991

When John Keel wrote ("Beyond the Known," FATE, March 1990) that the object which crashed in Roswell, New Mexico, more than 40 years ago was probably a World War II Japanese Fugo balloon bomb, howls were heard throughout the UFO community. Specifically, some people who have written books and are lecturing on UFOs—and especially on the idea that the object that crashed at Roswell in 1947 was an alien vehicle—disagreed. We gave them a chance to give their comments in an article ("The Roswell Furor," FATE, January 1991) and let John Keel respond to those comments. Even so, the article ruffled enough feathers that there was a demand for one more—and final—article on the subject at this time. To try and be fair, both of the following writers were given the same amount of space, and their articles are virtually unedited. Neither writer had the chance to see the other's comments.

All of the columns in FATE are the opinions of the writers. The article that appeared in January 1991 was also the opinion of its writers. So, too, are the opinions given in the following article. They are not necessarily the opinions of

FATE. FATE would like to make the following corrections to opinions which previously appeared: 1) Mr. Friedman has earned only part of his living for over two decades by lecturing about the ETH (extraterrestrial hypothesis) and UFOs. 2) Contrary to Mr. Keel's claim, Mr. Friedman claims that he presents both the ETH and the anti-ETH in his lectures and books. However, Mr. Friedman's basic focus is pro-ETH. 3) Although Mr. Friedman has not been a member of the government or armed forces, he has worked on classified government sponsored research and development activities for 14 years at five companies, visited different research and development facilities and spent "weeks" at government archives. 4) Robert Goddard did not work in Aztec, New Mexico, as written by Mr. Keel. He did his rocket research in Roswell, New Mexico.

The first writer is Stanton T. Friedman who is a lecturer on UFOs and "a major contributor" to the book *The Roswell Incident* by Charles Berlitz and William Moore. Because we are not censoring anything he wrote, some of our readers might be a bit confused—a few of his comments refer to information and articles that appeared elsewhere. He stresses that his information comes from numerous interviews.

The Real Roswell Story
By Stanton T. Friedman

I would never have believed that more than 15 years after my first conversation with Lydia Sleppy about a crashed saucer in New Mexico, that I would still be pursuing the biggest story of the century, the recovery of at least two crashed saucers in New Mexico in July 1947. It has been a long, rewarding, and sometimes frustrating quest. Some key people have died. Others remain to be found. But there is no question that there is overwhelming evidence that at two different sites, about 160 miles apart, two different sets of wreckage were recovered by the U.S. government. Many witnesses, civilian and military, were strongly intimidated by government agents.

Despite the initial official press release about recovery of a crashed disc, the weather balloon radar reflector cover story was successful right from the beginning about the Brazel ranch site 75 miles Northwest of Roswell. It effectively threw a blanket in the morning newspapers of July 9, 1947, over the crashed disc story that made it into many evening papers on July 8. It came from General Roger Ramey, Head of the 8th Air Force based in Ft. Worth, Texas, of which the 509th Composite Bomb Wing stationed at Roswell was a very important part.

Naturally the noisy negativists have been attacking the story almost from the first time it surfaced in my documentary movie *UFOs Are Real* in 1979 and in the 1980 book to which I was a major contributor *The Roswell Incident* (Berlitz and Moore). Moore, whom I had brought into the picture, and I had done 95 percent of the research, but the book included a great deal of undocumented material from Berlitz and had essentially no public impact. By 1985 Moore and I had published six more papers. The number of directly involved witnesses had increased from 60 to 90 but except for a small community of UFO buffs, most people were blissfully unaware of the story.

The treatment in the tabloid TV movie *UFO Cover-Up? Live!* in October of 1988 did little to help the cause even though it included brief appearances by Moore, heavily involved in its production, myself, and Jesse Marcel, M.D., son of Major Jesse Marcel (Intelligence Officer for the 509th) who had with his father, handled pieces of the wreckage. Dr. Marcel is a pilot and has served on a number of military aircraft accident investigative teams and is well qualified indeed to evaluate the strange wreckage and the very unusual symbols, not Japanese, seen on some of the pieces of very lightweight, very strong wreckage. Probably what most recall is the Falcon and Condor nonsense about strawberry ice cream and the bits and pieces from early science-fiction movies—ugh!

This sad spectacle led me to give up on letting Moore and Berlitz control the release of the story that I had worked so hard on, as the first to talk not only to Sleppy who tried to put the phoned-in story from Roswell on the Newswire from radio station KOA in Albuquerque, but to Major Marcel and to Vern and Jean Maltais who told of their good friend Barney Barnett's story of being next to a crashed, essentially intact saucer with alien bodies in the Plains of San Augustine in New Mexico, in the late 1940s. I pushed very hard, apparently successfully, to get the producers of *Unsolved Mysteries* to do the story and helped find some of the people they used besides being on briefly myself. The show ranked 12th on September 20, 1989, and seventh for the week on January 24, 1990, being seen by more than 30 million people. Many new witnesses came forth with bits and pieces of the story. Essentially none were aware of the book or our early papers or the movie scenes with Jesse. New flight-crew members came forth as did many others.

Of special interest was Gerald Anderson of Missouri who had been at the Barnett site with his brother, uncle, father and cousin, and touched one of the alien bodies before the archaeological group showed up just before the military came along in usual threatening fashion. He made site drawings after a hypnosis session with John Carpenter, a psychiatric social worker who was trained at the Menninger Clinic and has used hypnosis, in this case for memory enhancement, for a decade. Thanks to a sponsor, John and I and Gerald and my co-author Don Berliner, an old hand at ufology, were able to locate the actual site matching the drawing with a location in New Mexico even to the windmill that was indeed there.

A very active and initially independent effort to evaluate the Roswell incident has also been conducted by Don Schmitt of the Center for UFO Studies and former Air Force Captain Kevin Randle, initially a skeptic. Don had asked me if there was more to do. I gave an enthusiastic "yes," but pointed out that I could not afford to spend the money on phone calls and travel that was required. When I was hot and heavy on Roswell in 1979, my phone bills frequently ran over $500 per month as they have most months the past 2 years. Don S. and Kevin R. have found many more crew members and have made many trips to New Mexico. They have a book due out this year as do Don Berliner and I. We all cooperated on a project with the Fund for UFO Research that involved bringing witnesses to Washington, D.C., for a closed conference. I and either Kevin or

Don Schmitt jointly interviewed and taped other important witnesses unable to go to D.C.

Not surprisingly the noisy negativists have had their knives out since 1980 and are still attacking. Noisy negativism has been characterized as one might expect by an almost complete lack of investigation, by ad hominem attacks, by proclamations, by false reasoning, by very selective choice of data. These tricks of the propagandists have characterized the intellectual bankruptcy of anti-ufology for decades. Book reviewers attacked *The Roswell Incident* for the garbage and conveniently ignored the good stuff. Even earlier, Ted Bloecher in his book on the 1947 UFO wave had dismissed the Roswell story though not getting it right. Frank Edwards in *Flying Saucers Serious Business* used one paragraph, mostly factually in error, to pretty much dismiss the story. Neither of the two UFO encyclopedias published around 1980 even mentioned the story. Phil Klass [of CSICOP, the Committee for Skeptical Investigation of Claims of the Paranormal] naturally made more than 20 factual misstatements in a three-page treatment of Roswell in his book *UFOs: The Public Deceived* as I have noted in my 1985 paper "Flying Saucers, Noisy Negativists and Truth." Klass had, of course, not talked to any of the witnesses, reviewed none of the evidence and hadn't been to Roswell or the Plains of San Augustine. Henry Gordon of Canada viciously attacked the story and me in articles in the Toronto Star. Naturally he had done no research.

John Keel is the latest to jump on the anti-Roswell bandwagon. As with Klass and Gordon, he has talked to none of the witnesses, not been on the scene, ignored all the published data, and made proclamations totally unverified by any documentation. The bashers have, of course, completely ignored the fact that the 509th was the only atomic bombing group in the world, that the stories taken independently have been consistent including testimony from General Thomas Jefferson DuBose, General Ramey's chief of staff who was told directly to cover up the story by the SAC (Strategic Air Command) boss in D.C.

Perhaps out of a perverted sense of humor, Keel has tried to convert a load of small pieces of wreckage almost weightless but extraordinarily strong into a Japanese Fugo balloon somehow with witnesses supposedly stimulated by rockets launched by Robert Goddard in Aztec, New Mexico, which was also the site of supposed crashes described by Frank Scully in his long-dismissed book, *Behind the Flying Saucers*. Keel's sole contribution seems to have been a possible phone conversation with an unnamed historian in Roswell in the 1960s. He claims the story was revived by loads of UFO buffs periodically beating the bushes in Roswell and that all accounts tell of brown paper as the main constituent. Great science-fiction debunking but without a shred of supporting evidence.

Unfortunately for Keel's attempts to somehow mix in Scully, whose sources were con men Newton and Gebauer, as opposed to the myriad of legitimate military men and local witnesses involved in the event as have been found by my colleagues and myself along with loads of newspaper stories, Goddard worked in Roswell not in Aztec which is 300 miles way from Roswell. Not only is there newspaper coverage of the original official Army/Air Force story (naturally ignored by Keel), but there is an FBI memo that Keel casually dismisses as having been done for the amusement of J. Edgar Hoover. The man who wrote the memo refused to talk to Bill Moore when visited and had been instructed not to say anything.

One way to judge the validity of the critics is to note their past accuracy. Klass, for example, claimed that the tradition at the White House in 1954 was the use of small elite type whereas a memo supposedly dealing with Operation Majestic 12 (ostensibly set up to deal with the Roswell crash) was in large pica type ... and therefore presumably a fraud. He loudly offered me $100 for each genuine memo done in the same size and style pica type used in the memo but set a limit of ten. I did indeed collect $1,000 for providing many more than 10. The point is how could Klass, who had never been to the Eisenhower library make such an outlandish claim, in view of the 250,000 pages of NSC material at the library, on the basis of 9 items There are many other "Klassical" boners easily avoidable with real research

Keel, too, has recently about UFOs. He falsely claimed that the MJ–12 documents were frauds because all government documents of that vintage were done on 8" x 10" paper. I have visited a total of 14 archives and saw plenty of 8.5" x 11" paper. He claimed that many books in the '60s noted MJ–12 when in fact he was referring to the 5412 committee, which only had a few members, not 12, and dealt with covert activities. No connection. He claimed that J. Edgar Hoover saw to it that no Jews received high level security clearances in the mid 1950s—another laugher since I am Jewish and received an AEC Q clearance in 1956.

He claimed I made a fool of myself by claiming that plutonium is used in atom bombs when it isn't. Funny, the first two atom bombs indeed used plutonium as the fissionable material. Our massive plutonium production facilities make it for bombs. He claimed I was spending full time lecturing about UFOs when since 1982 I have been mixing scientific work as a nuclear physicist with ufology.

This small list should give ample demonstration that Keel's undocumented proclamations, like Klass's, cannot be believed. He hasn't even been able to show that any Fugo balloons (as opposed to various weather balloons) were ever recovered in New Mexico even during the war as opposed to 2 years after. Considering the wind directions and the many mountain ranges that is not surprising. He has provided not one article, no less all articles, saying the main material was brown paper and has not given the name of any witness he interviewed (we have named dozens) and no evidence of supposedly frequent reviving of the story by UFO buffs prior to my first interview with Major Marcel. I heard of Marcel through Don Allan, a TV station manager who was a ham radio buddy of Marcel. Neither was seeking attention. The evidence is overwhelming. There are indeed crashed saucers in U.S. possession.

The second writer is John Keel—author, lecturer and writer on the paranormal and Fortean phenomena. His arguments are based on interdisciplinary research into a variety of fields.

Roswell's Last Gasp
By John A. Keel

There is an old country saying that states: "If it looks like a skunk and smells like a skunk, it is almost assuredly a skunk."

Over the years, many people have written to me about Roswell and I have always told them the same thing: i.e., first read chapter 4 of Charles Berlitz's book *The Roswell Incident* carefully. Then read any of the many books and articles available about the Japanese World War II bomb-carrying Fugo balloons, noting the details of how they were constructed and what they were made of. Then go back and read Berlitz again.

It's that simple.

The Roswell interviewees all described the debris found on the New Mexico ranch as being largely made of paper marked with Oriental symbols or writing. They even emphasized these two points! The Fugo balloons, you will find, were made of very special paper, laminated in four layers, that was almost impossible to tear and couldn't even be cut with scissors. Most of it was bluish on one side and silvery on the other (to reflect the heat of the sun).

It has always been easy to dismiss the Berlitz book because it is totally lacking in documentation and is heavily padded with many of the most notorious hoaxes in the UFO cult literature, particularly some the late Gray Barker's best hoaxes (he was an inveterate practical joker who enjoyed stirring up the UFO buffs).

A large part of the problem is that Mr. Berlitz, my old luncheon companion and a very busy man, innocently relied on two ardent UFO bibliophiles who totally lacked a basic background in journalism and psychology, essential subjects for this type of investigation. Interviewing people, especially people who are trying to recall events from many decades earlier, is an art that requires considerable training and experience. This duo was also plainly uninformed in such basics as aviation history, metallurgy and fundamental field research methods.

If you own a copy of the Berlitz book, dig it out and follow along with me. First of all, the ages of the participants are completely ignored. Age is a very important piece of documentation. Look at any newspaper story and you will find the age is always given. There are good reasons for this. For example, Charles Smith, 94, tells you a lot about Mr. Smith, as does Charles Smith, 12. When you are dealing with a very old event you absolutely must give the age of each person quoted. It is a bottom rule of journalism.

In the case of Roswell, age becomes one of the most important factors. You will note that Chapter Four gives few ages, or any other journalistically necessary personal information about any of the interviewees. The interviewers cannot be accused of being overly perceptive.

Secondly, we have the problem of hearsay. For some peculiar reason, UFO buffs have a hard time understanding the nature of hearsay. Ask any lawyer friend or any professional journalist and you will find out why hearsay is totally unacceptable in any subject.

Unfortunately, the entire Roswell case is built on hearsay. That is, people are trying to recall what someone else told them many years earlier. In some instances, they are trying to recall what someone told someone who told someone who then told them! Can you, yourself, recall in any detail a casual conversation you may have had with someone 30 years ago? Of course, you can't. That's why no judge and no newspaper editor would allow your hearsay recollections to be entered into the record. As I said, it takes a very highly trained interviewer to even attempt to handle such material, and Berlitz's dynamic duo had no such qualifications.

There are so many correlations between the Fugo balloons and the Roswell debris that one could write a book about them, even using the amateurish material developed in the Berlitz tome. For example, one in every 24 balloons carried a cleverly designed tracking radio. The Japanese built three special radio stations to try to receive the signals from these radios and thus pinpoint the locations of the balloons. The radios were very, very light, for obvious reasons, and contained no tubes. Through an ingenious system of coils and condensers they sent out a brief signal once each hour. This was to conserve their very limited battery power. The radios looked like black boxes and were so finely crafted that once they were assembled they could not easily be opened again. Sort of like the famous Oriental trick boxes that we are all acquainted with.

In Frank Scully's 1950 book *Behind the Flying Saucers*, he specifically mentions one of these radios—more than once—claiming he was shown one of them that had been found in New Mexico. Repeat: found in New Mexico. In fact, these little radios and their hourly signals are discussed in much of the early UFO literature, always with the assumption that they were otherworldly. In Berlitz's Roswell book (on page 65 there) we learn that a man identified only as "Cavitt" found a mysterious black box in all the Oriental-inscribed paper at Roswell, couldn't figure out how to open it and tossed it onto a truck with the rest of the debris. As shallow and incomplete as the Berlitz interviews are, there is enough material to indicate that everything found at Roswell was Fugo-related—silken shroud lines, etc. There is absolutely nothing in the descriptions to relate the debris with what we know about UFOs.

Normal investigative procedure in any event such as a plane crash, crime (particularly murder) and even archaeological digs, is to first photograph everything in site before touching it. Then each piece is numbered and cataloged, noting its exact position in relation to the other pieces. Only after this has been done are the pieces carefully picked up, measured, etc., and packed away. This standard procedure was followed at many of the Fugo crash sites around the country (the balloons turned up as far east as Michigan) but it was not done at Roswell. So there was absolutely no documentation of the actual debris site. Repeat: there was absolutely no documentation of the debris site. The clearly disinterested Air Force officers just scooped the stuff into trucks and carried it off. As soon as it was picked up it became instant junk. The only surviving documentation on Roswell consists of two yellowing newspaper clippings and some photos taken by a newspaperman. The photos show officers fondling some sheets of pliable silver material that resembles exactly the paper used in the Fugo balloons. The photographer is said to have remembered that it smelled "like burning rubber" which, not surprisingly, is what the Fugos smelled like. They were heavily treated with a special chemical derived from a Japanese plant, an adhesive similar to rubber cement.

Author Charles Berlitz paid the two interviewers hard cash for their tapes, etc. They have since extracted more money from novelist Whitley Strieber, the Fund for UFO Research and others for this poorly compiled, very questionable and completely undocumented material. Roswell has proven to be a very profitable enterprise. In recent months, the various participants have been feuding with each other, threatening lawsuits and claiming ownership of the story. (Since Roswell was a news event, no one owns it. The various interviewees own their remembrances, not the interviewers.)

Berlitz has washed his hands of the whole affair and ended his relationships with the two interviewers years ago, citing "character differences." After writing a flop novel, *Majestic*, based on the Roswell myth, Mr. Strieber has abandoned the UFO field in dismay, disgusted with the antics of the malicious ufologists whom he has defined in a public letter as "the cruelest, nastiest, and craziest people I have ever encountered."

A novelist named Kevin Randle has re-interviewed those who allegedly knew the Roswell rancher and viewed the debris and has published a book, *UFO Crash at Roswell*, which attempts to link the Roswell debris with the legendary bodies of little men described by Scully and immortalized in Gray Barker's *Hangar 18* hoax and other cultist material.

So the story goes on. Interestingly, very few UFO buffs bothered to visit their libraries and read about the Japanese

Fugo project after I brought it up. Instead, they have filled their little newsletters with childish personal attacks against me and amazing dissections of my prose. Although I was careful to repeat the main points over and over in my rather brief FATE response to their earlier emotional tirades, they ignored the key points and tried to debate the meaning of words. Perhaps if they had a Ph.D. in English literature such a debate would be meaningful but none of them are qualified to engage in a discussion of semantics. One cult magazine published on the West Coast went so far as to rewrite my FATE article about the Fugos and then put my name on it, apparently assuming (wrongly) this was the way to get around FATE's copyright. Then, incredibly, the Roswell advocates wasted their time and paper "analyzing" the bogus article and attacking me for what it did or did not contain!

I did not even know about the article until many weeks after it was published. Others have assaulted the typographical errors, which I have absolutely no control over. To save them further effort, let me state my conclusions as succinctly as possible: The Roswell affair is an easily provable misinterpretation with no link whatsoever with flying saucers. The people who perpetrated this on Mr. Berlitz, Mr. Strieber and others in my opinion were either motivated by greed or by sheer stupidity. Or maybe by both. Considering all that has happened in the last few years, the circulation of falsified documents, etc., "misinterpretation" is no longer an appropriate word. It has become a major hoax—and a criminal hoax. Since a great deal of money has changed hands because of it, it can now be classified legally as grand larceny and there are severe penalties for that. The deliberate faking of government documents can result in a 20-year jail term.

Many aviation historians (they have a large national organization) devoted years of their lives to documenting and studying the Japanese Fugo project, preparing detailed catalogs of where the balloons came down, etc. The Smithsonian Institution had a Fugo on display for years and in 1990 published a new edition of their little souvenir booklet about the balloons. You can obtain it from the Government Printing Office or the Smithsonian. There are other editions available from aviation book clubs and bookstores. Chances are there is even an active aviation historian in your area who will be glad to read chapter four of your copy of the Berlitz book and give you his independent opinion of it.

This is simply a case of something that looked like a Fugo, and smelled like a Fugo and was turned into a UFO by a couple of overeager saucer enthusiasts. It was accepted blindly, without question by that small but hardy band who live by what writers call "suspension of disbelief" and it has now acquired religious-like significance. Contrary to the assertions of the amateurs, there were no witnesses in 1947—that is, no one actually saw the debris come down. The man who found the debris on his ranch after a storm died in 1963 and was never properly interviewed by anyone before his death. But this is no longer a case for amateur ufologists. It is a case for the proper legal authorities and the courts.

Is this truly a "Roswell Finale?" For FATE it is, at least for now. The main problem with this affair is that it happened over four decades ago, and as our poll reported in our July issue (in "I See By the Papers"), relatively few people were interested enough to write in and comment about what our writers had said. Some who wrote in gave their own pre-established opinions rather than commenting on the January article.

We at FATE believe the subject has been covered. We will not be printing more on it until some tangible evidence becomes available.

FATE is taking no position on what crashed at Roswell. We can say that we are sure that something crashed there. Unfortunately, reviewing books and newspapers or listening to the memories that people have of 44 years ago will not resolve the problem. Writing to FATE or strictly UFO-oriented magazines will not help, either. What will help is massive letter writing to your Federal representatives in Congress to reveal all of the information—including any remaining physical evidence —they have on the object that crashed at Roswell. Until they reveal this information, anything further on the subject is moot.

UFO Chronicles
Special Guest Columnist: James McWilliams
July 1997

For 50 years, ufologists have been fascinated by the mystery that started at 9:50 p.m on July 2, 1947, in Roswell, New Mexico.

That's when the Wilmot family first reported a "big glowing object … like two inverted saucers faced mouth-to-mouth." They said the object shot across the sky from the southeast to the northwest.

During an electrical storm that evening, W. W. "Mac" Brazel and two of his children heard something like an explosion. He assumed it had been thunder—until the next day when Mac found unusual wreckage scattered over a quarter-mile-long stretch of his land. Six days later, Lt. Walter Haut at the Roswell Army Air Base informed the press that base intelligence officer Maj. Jesse A. Marcel had picked up the remains of a flying disk that had crashed at an area ranch. The news received international publicity.

The military quickly recanted, saying the debris recovered at Roswell came from a weather device. Over the years, Marcel and other eyewitnesses have claimed otherwise. Numerous books and articles have attempted to shed light on the subject, but the best way to learn about the alleged UFO cover-up is to go there yourself.

Here's a quick guide to five must-see spots in Roswell:

International UFO Museum

Deon Crosby has the right qualifications for her new job as the director of the International UFO Museum and Research Center in Roswell: She has actually seen UFOs.

"I was driving toward Roswell from Vaughn between 10 p.m. and midnight," she said, "when I saw four rotating lights toward the Roswell horizon. They rotated around me in a peculiar pattern and motion. I saw something that I was unable to identify."

Crosby, who became the museum's director in May 1996, places great credence in the findings of researchers such as Stanton Friedman, Leonard Stringfield, and Linda Moulton Howe. "The strongest evidence, I believe," she said, "is the personal witness of the people I know to be credible."

The museum opened on September 27, 1991, with the collaboration of Walter Haut, Glenn Dennis, and Max Littell. Haut was the public relations officer who wrote and released the Roswell incident story. Dennis was the mortician who became involved in the incident at the base hospital, and Max Littell was the business partner who helped crystallize the venture. The museum is located in the Plains Theater at 114 North Main in Roswell. Opposition to the museum has been prominent in some quarters. "In the '60s, the mayor of this town basically mandated that nothing related to UFOs would be connected to Roswell," Deon said. "He didn't want Roswell to become, as he called it, 'kook city.'"

Today, the museum is recognized and supported by the current mayor and local residents. In 1996, the Tourism Association of New Mexico presented the museum with the Top Tourist Destination of New Mexico Award. The new museum boasts exhibits covering all aspects of the 1947 Roswell incident plus other exhibits on space, crop circles, abductions, cattle mutilations, and ancient cultures.

The North Impact Site

About 30 miles north of Roswell on Highway 285, a sign marks a turn to the west. If you travel about eight miles west from the turnoff, you will find the North Impact Site, also known as the Kaufman Site.

Herbert Miller "Hub" Corn is the proud owner of this piece of UFO history, something he discovered when he took over the family farm. He noticed people driving around on his land and wondered what they were doing. Finally, he asked a state police officer and learned that they were searching for the site where a UFO came down in July 1947.

People sometimes take property from the site without his permission, Hub said. "A guy called the museum three or four months ago trying to sell them dirt from the impact site. I told them to get his number so I could see where my real estate was going."

Hub will take visitors to the site for a $15 fee, because he says the tours cut into his principal livelihood, ranching and farming. People come from all 50 states and several foreign countries to visit the site. Even celebrities come for the tour. "We had Jonathan Frakes (star of *Star Trek: The Next Generation*), some of David Letterman's crew, and an assortment of writers and songwriters," he recalled.

Hub gives visitors an information sheet titled "On the Roswell Crash Impact Site." Written by noted UFO author Kevin Randle, it explains why Hub's property is considered the site of the famous UFO impact. Many people—including Frank Kaufman and Major Edwin Easley—claim to have seen the crashed UFO on Hub's property.

The West Impact Site

Less well known than the North Site, the West Site surfaced in 1993 when Max Littell of the International UFO Museum and Research Center in Roswell visited James Ragsdale at the request of an author. Ragsdale told of a UFO crash in the nearby Lincoln National Forest that he and a friend had witnessed. Five days before his death on July 1, 1995, he signed an affidavit to set the record straight.

He said that he and a female friend were camped off Arabella Road near Boy Scout Mountain (about 53 miles west of Roswell) on Friday, July 4, 1947. At about 11:30 p.m., they saw a flash, and then a flaming craft came toward them from the north. It crashed within 60 yards of their truck.

Examination of the crash that night and the next morning revealed a saucer-shaped craft about 20 feet in diameter with a dome in the middle. The craft had struck two large boulders and split open near the bottom.

Ragsdale described the four dead bodies inside as strange-looking "little people" less than four feet tall. The craft's interior, he said, was fascinating—both in its workmanship and in its beauty.

Ragsdale's story has caused some researchers to postulate that two extraterrestrial craft collided near Corona, New Mexico. One craft, saucer-shaped, crashed near Boy Scout Mountain west of Roswell. The other, a bat-shaped craft, crashed north of Roswell. While eyewitness testimony at the North Site is well documented, researchers hope other witnesses will be able to corroborate Ragsdale's story.

Directions to the West Impact Site can be picked up at the International UFO Museum and Research Center.

Hangar 84

Anyone paying a visit to Roswell should be sure to see Hangar 84 off of east Enterprise Street in the Roswell Industrial Air Park. The park is in southern Roswell and was formerly Roswell Army Air Field, later named Walker Air Force Base. One can view the hangar's exterior without permission, but to go inside requires permission from Renown Aviation.

Back in 1947, this hangar was known as hangar P–3 and was reputed to have been the temporary storage site of UFO wreckage and alien bodies. Witnesses stated that the bodies were packed in dry ice and stored in a large crate placed in the middle of the empty hangar. Military police surrounded the perimeter, both inside and outside the building, to ensure security.

Supposedly, on Monday, July 7, 1947, at 2:00 a.m., under the cover of darkness, the bodies and materials were secretly loaded onto two separate aircraft. One of them headed for Fort Worth Army Air Field. From there, the cargo was taken to other military installations for inspection by high-ranking military and civilian authorities.

One witness, Frank Kaufman, reported that the bodies were flown out in two separate flights to guard against all of them being lost in one accident. The second aircraft was routed directly to Wright Army Air Field.

Hangar 84 is the famous hangar where Oliver Wendell "Pappy" Henderson allegedly viewed the UFO wreckage and bodies before flying them on to their individual destinations and places in UFO history.

The Enigma UFO Museum

In 1987, John Arnold Price and his wife, Sherron, opened the Outa' Limits Video Store. Since Price was interested in the Roswell UFO incident, he decided to put some displays in his store window concerning MJ–12, the 1952 document that purportedly informed President Eisenhower that the U.S. government had recovered two crashed UFOs, and established the secret "Majestic–12" group to deal with "extraterrestrial biological entities."

The store became a hot spot for UFO researchers and Roswell witnesses. Price's own interest deepened; and he researched the phenomenon further, adding new displays to the store.

In 1990, UFO skeptic Phil Klass debated Clifford Stone, a local UFO researcher at the store. Store traffic was heavy that night and interfered with the videotaping of the debate. Later, when the problem repeated itself during an interview of Glenn Dennis, the mortician involved with the Roswell incident, Price decided to separate the UFO displays and video store. So, in April 1992, he officially opened the UFO Enigma Museum.

The Roswell crash scene in the Blue Room is one if visitors' favorite displays. It depicts a crashed saucer with three dead aliens and one live one in the custody of an army M.P

Other displays feature photos and artifacts of UFOs, both stateside and overseas.

Researchers and authors Kevin Randle, Donald Schmitt, and Stanton Friedman have visited the museum. Celebrities and politicians have also dropped in, but Price says the latter keep a low profile.

THREE: Close Encounters and Contactees

By close encounters, we mean specifically instances where witnesses actually see the inhabitants of a UFO up close and personal, perhaps even conversing with them, but without necessarily being carried off by them. According to the traditional classification system, this would be Close Encounters of the Third Kind. Beyond merely seeing the occupant of a UFO, there is the experience of actually talking to them, being taken for a ride by them, or being kidnapped by them for unknown purposes. They can be friendly, as when they offer advice about the value of Vedanta or the misuse of atomic energy, or they can behave like physicians with horrible bedside manners, taciturn, professional, and just plain weird.

As a prime example of meeting a bug-eyed monster up close and personal, there is Gray Barker's hair-raising account of the Flatwoods Monster—see it and run. But here also is an early article by George Adamski, before his 1953 book about hobnobbing with Venusians from a landed spacecraft, concerning the relatively mundane activity of photographing spaceships. The usual opinion is that his UFOs are actually lampshades, but that could be debated. Meanwhile, his adventures with his extraterrestrial friends, still in the future when this article was written, were almost certainly astral in nature and did not take place in physical reality—not unless the nature of the solar system has changed dramatically in the last 50 years. One currently popular view is that he faked it all in order to promulgate his New Age Eastern philosophy and teachings, which could never gain any acceptance or popularity on their own without being put into the mouths of beings from other worlds. Were his contacts alien astronauts, or his psychic spiritual teachers?

The Monster and the Saucer
By Gray Barker

January 1953

On September 12, 1952, the nation's wire services crackled with news of a 10-foot, red-faced monster, which sprayed a foul, sickening gas and frightened seven Flatwoods, West Virginia, residents into panic.

"It looked worse than Frankenstein," Mrs. Kathleen May, one of a party who climbed a hill to investigate a flying saucer sighting, told reporters.

Shortly afterward I went to Flatwoods, a small town of 300, and spent three days subjecting these seven people, and other residents of the area, to rigorous questioning. If this story were true, I felt it deserved factual reporting; if it were a hoax I wished to explode it.

The stories obtained from the seven different persons who had been present were heard separately. Although their accounts did not reach the terrifying proportions originally reported, and some of them had taken on color through retellings and leading questions, their stories agreed, except in very minor details. And try as I might, I could not break these stories down.

On that terrifying night reports of strange lights and objects in the skies were prevalent from Ohio eastward to Washington D.C., and from Virginia northward to Pennsylvania. About seven o'clock, just as it had become dark, Mrs. May, a beautician, was told by her two small sons, Eddie 13, and Fred 12, that they had seen a "flying saucer" land on a hilltop above their house. The two May children had been at a nearby playground with Gene Lemon 17, Neil Nunley 14, Ronnie Shaver 10, and Tommy Hyer, also 10.

The "saucer" which the children described to me, "looked like a silver dollar rushing through the sky," spouting an exhaust which looked like red balls of fire. It came southwestward across the sky and, directly over the hilltop, paused, seemed to hover, and descended out of view on the other side.

The group ran to Mrs. May's home, at the base of the hill, and the two May children told their mother about the object. She insisted it was "just their imaginations," until she looked upward and saw a strange red glow. Gene Lemon found a flashlight and led the party up the hill after Mrs. May agreed to accompany them.

Although not definitely timed, not more than a half-hour could have elapsed from the time of the sighting and the moment Lemon screamed with terror and fell backward, and the party fled from the sight before them.

I am now listening to tape-recorded interviews, correlating details, and sifting out those that do not exactly agree or might be colored by the horror and excitement of the moment.

The story told with least emotion is that of Neil Nunley, and the exact words I will quote will be his. Nunley impressed me as being a very levelheaded and unimaginative youngster. He was very definite on what he saw and what he did not see.

He and Lemon were ahead of the others. Before them, up a roadway leading to the hilltop, they could see a reddish light pulsating from dim to bright. As they approached, they encountered a mist that resembled fog but which carried a pungent, irritating odor. It seemed to become denser as they walked farther.

As they went over the hilltop, through a gateway, they saw a globular object down over the hill to their right, about 50 feet away.

"It was just a big ball of fire," Nunley explained, and it would grow dimmer and brighter at regular intervals. He could not estimate the exact size, but others in the party said it was "big as a house."

Because their attentions were on the globe they did not notice a huge figure standing to their left, near the hilltop, until they were about 15 feet from it. Seeing two glowing green spots, which he thought were animal eyes, Lemon turned his flashlight in that direction.

Towering above them was a man-like shape. Its face was round, and blood-red. Around the face was a pointed hood-like shape, dark in appearance. In the "face" were two eye-like openings from which greenish-orange" beams projected over their heads. The body, illuminated by the flashlight from the head downward to the waist, appeared dark and colorless to Nunley, although some others said it was green. Mrs. May said she saw clothing-like folds around the figure. Descriptions from the waist down are vague; most of the seven said this part of the figure was not under view.

Not all agreed that the "monster" had arms. Mrs. May described it with terrible claws. Some said they just didn't see any. Not all agreed on the height of the figure, but according to their descriptions it couldn't have been more than 10 feet tall. It was said to have stood under an over-hanging limb about 15 feet from the ground, and it didn't reach to this limb.

A powerful odor, described by all as sickening and irritating to the nostrils, pervaded the scene. Some had originally said it smelled like burning metal or burning sulphur, but under questioning none of the seven could remember anything in their experiences resembling the odor.

Others in the party reported a sound, coming either from the figure or the globular object, described as something between a hiss and a high-pitched squeal. They could also hear a thumping or throbbing noise.

The figure was observed for a very short while, a matter of seconds, because of the terror they experienced. It was impossible to ascertain the exact length of time it was viewed; most of the stories varied slightly. But all agreed with Nunley that it was "a very short time. We just got a good look at it and left."

The figure was moving toward them but inscribing an arc, which, after viewing the scene, I estimate would lead the entity down the hillside to the globular object.

I questioned Nunley at length about the means of locomotion employed by the figure. I asked him to re-enact the scene and walk about, imitating it.

"I couldn't move as it did. It just moved. It didn't walk. It moved evenly; it didn't jump."

He could still view the figure after Lemon screamed and dropped the flashlight. The globular shape, he explained, emitted enough light to make the figure visible.

Two of the party, Mrs. May and Lemon, said they did not see the globe. They were the worst frightened, however, and their entire attention may have been centered on the figure. The Nunley boy was very definite about the globe, though; he said the reason they got so close to the monster before seeing it was because they were looking at the globe.

They had taken a dog with them, and Nunley said it howled and ran away and was found at the house with "its tail tucked between its legs."

At the house they telephoned the nearby town of Sutton, the Braxton County seat, for law officials but were told that Sheriff Robert Carr and his deputy were near Frame-town, another small town about 17 miles southward, investigating the report of a plane crash. About an hour later they returned to Sutton, heard of the Flatwoods incident, and rushed to the scene. They climbed the hill, investigated, but saw, heard and smelled nothing.

I questioned A. Lee Stewart, Jr., of the Braxton (W.Va.) Democrat, who arrived shortly before the sheriff, and found some members of the party receiving first aid. Others were too terrified to talk coherently. He finally was able to persuade Lemon to accompany him to the hilltop.

No signs of the figure or globe were visible, but bending close to the ground he could smell the strange odor, which he also described as sickening and irritating. He said he had smelled gases used in warfare, while in the Air Force, but had encountered nothing similar.

At seven o'clock the next morning he returned and found "skid marks" in the tall grass, leading from the spot where the figure was seen to where the globe was reported. The earth was not disturbed, but small stones had been tossed aside.

I have been over the site carefully. I saw marks and a huge area of grass trampled down, but multitudes have visited and walked over the location. I believe Stewart's observations are accurate, however. I could see no trace of the oil reported to have been present on the ground and to have saturated the weeds with an odd, gummy deposit; but there had been a rain. Some said samples of the deposit were being analyzed but I could not track down the information.

Although Flatwoods residents shake their heads and discredit the story, attributing the phenomena to anything from a buck deer with white breast to the dome of the State House; allegedly stolen and flown to Washington by the party in power, there have arisen dozens of variations, each more hair-raising than the other before.

I ran down a number of rumors. I drove 50 miles to interview a man who had claimed to be present when a space ship had taken off from the hill. He told me he had not seen this occur, but had been present shortly after the incident and seen an object in the air. It was round, with a flat top, orange in color. Streams of fire, like jets, were projecting downward from the apex. He agreed to meet me that evening, drive to Flatwoods with me and point out the exact spot over which the object had circled and then flew south-westward. He did not keep the appointment.

Numerous people in a 20-mile radius saw illuminated objects in the sky at the same time. I could have spent a month interviewing all of such viewers. The objects were described mainly as round, red or orange in color, and spouting fire.

These objects were reported flying in various directions, although the progress of some of them could be charted. It is evident that either they saw different objects, or one object was making a circuit of the area.

Mayor J. Holt Burne of Sutton, also editor of his Braxton Central, put the inevitable question to me.

"Well, what do *you* think it was?"

Sitting in his newspaper office, surrounded by the hustle and bustle of a busy small town, I should have liked to say, "The misinterpretation of natural phenomena."

In my belief, I told him, the account fits perfectly with others of flying saucers or similar craft.

I believe that such a vehicle landed on the hillside, either from necessity or to make observations.

The monster could have been a robot from the globular ship, or some entity inside a suit that would adapt the wearer to Earth's atmosphere. When the flashlight was shone upon it, that stimulus then would start the creature on its way back to the ship. Or perhaps it did not see nor take notice of the seven odd bipeds that had come to view it and, had they waited, might have completed its progress to the ship and left.

But that is speculation. What I do know is that when you talk to seven people with honesty and fear in their eyes, you know in your heart when they are telling the truth. These people did see *something*. And whatever they saw was very much like what they described.

UFO Lands in New Mexico
By Coral Lorenzen

August 1964

Officer Lonnie Zamora had been chasing a car on Park Street in Socorro, New Mexico, at about 5:40 p.m. on Friday, April 24, 1964. Near the Church of La Buena Pastor (Good Shepherd) his attention was caught by a roaring sound and a blue flame southwest of him. In the area where the flash appeared there is a dynamite storage shack and Zamora feared there had been an explosion there. He radioed headquarters in Socorro and cut off Park Street onto a narrow winding trail among the hillocks and gullies in the direction of the shack.

As he descended a small rise and started into a wash he saw what he thought was an overturned car with its top exposed to him, about 450 feet away in a deep gully. Zamora radioed headquarters again from this point, since he assumed there had been an accident and a car was overturned.

To approach the overturned car Zamora would have to drive up out of the draw he was in onto a small mesa. As he looked further he saw what he later described as an egg-shaped, white object with two protrusions, like legs, and two man-shaped beings who appeared to be doing something to the object. The beings were dressed in white and one turned toward him.

Zamora drove up onto the mesa and got out of his car. The object was still in its original position. But almost immediately it started belching blue flame from its underside. An ear-splitting, pulsating roar filled the air. Zamora turned and ran, looking back over his shoulder at the object as it climbed to about 20 feet altitude, when the roar and flame ceased. It then proceeded southwest toward the Black Range, ascending as it flew at high speed. It was out of sight in seconds.

At this point Sgt. Sam Chavez drove upon the scene. He had been alerted by Zamora's radio calls and had jumped into his squad car in an attempt to locate him. Chavez later told me that he arrived within three minutes after the initial radio call.

He found Zamora standing by his car, appearing to be very upset. After a brief conversation the two men descended into the gully to examine the spot where the object had rested. A mesquite bush and some small weeds were charred and smoking.

This is the bare outline of what was to be the most exciting UFO report I ever have investigated.

Exactly 17 hours after the Zamora sighting took place I received a telephone call from Mr. Arlynn Bruer, news editor of the Alamogordo Daily News. Sgt. Sam Chavez is a longtime friend of Bruer's so when the story came in on the wire Bruer talked with Chavez by phone, then called me. I alerted Terry Clarke of radio station KALG in Alamogordo, New Mexico, and began checking the story through members of APRO in central and northern New Mexico. Every source urged Mr. Lorenzen and me to come over and verify it for ourselves. So at 5 o'clock on Saturday afternoon, less than 24 hours after the incident occurred, we steered our ponderous old Cadillac east out of Tucson, Arizona.

At 9 o'clock the next morning we arrived at police headquarters and were seated at a desk facing Sgt. M. Samuel Chavez, of the New Mexico State Police. He was just finishing an interview with an Associated Press reporter. We waited.

Sergeant Chavez is about 41 years old and has 15 years service with the state police behind him. His air of competence and attention to detail generates a feeling of confidence, and his precise way of stating facts is reassuring. It was he who filled in the background details and, along with Police Chief Polo Pineda, testified to the competence, honesty and integrity as well as the courage of the witness, Patrolman Lonnie Zamora.

"Lonnie is not a man to be easily frightened," Chavez told us. "That thing must have made an impression on him to scare him like it did." Chief Pineda, who rode out to the site of the landing with Chavez, Mr. Lorenzen, and me said simply, "Lonnie is a good man."

As we drove out to the site of the landing Chavez pointed out the place on Park Street where Zamora first had spotted the cone-shaped blue flame in the sky to the southwest. At that point Zamora had discontinued his pursuit of the speeder, whose identity he felt he knew anyway, to proceed in the direction of the flame because he feared that an explosion had taken place at the dynamite vault.

He described the flame as four times as long as its widest point and coming down in the vicinity of the vault. Just after the blue flame dropped out of sight the roaring sound ceased and a whining sound, which earlier may have been masked by the roar, was heard. Its frequency decreased rapidly to zero. By then Zamora had left Park Street and was making his run up a steep rocky incline to the mesa. Because of the steepness and condition of the trail he made three tries before topping the grade, then as he began descending the southwest slope he spotted the object in the gully. From his position he was looking across one gully and up into another, somewhat down at the object. Still in his automobile he saw the object, two of its "legs" or landing gear, and two small white-clad figures. One turned and looked in his direction. He said they appeared to be "small adults" or "boys."

At this point Zamora, as he drove toward the incline leading to the second mesa, lost sight of the object as it was obscured by the terrain. He parked his car and got out, accidentally dislodging his microphone as he did so. He automatically hung this back in its proper place, then took three steps toward the object. At that instant, it set up an ear-splitting roar.

He was thoroughly frightened. He did not know what he was observing and he was within 100 to 150 feet of the object. He turned and ran almost blindly, banging his leg on his car as he passed it and dislodging his sunglasses. He ran almost directly west across the second mesa and into the next gully. As he ran, he looked over his shoulder because he heard the roar diminishing. It was then he saw the brilliant blue cone-shaped flame again.

The object had risen until it now was about 20 feet above the top of the mesa. Then the flame shrank to nothing and the roar ceased. Once again Zamora heard the whining sound, which began at a high frequency, dropped rapidly to a low frequency, and faded out. The object flew silently up the gully, barely missed the top of the dynamite vault, and ascended rapidly at a shallow angle in the direction of the Perlite mine southwest of Socorro. A few seconds later Sergeant Chavez's car ground up the steep grade to the second mesa and stopped. Zamora walked over; the two men talked, then went to examine the gully where the strange machine had rested.

It is a dry, rocky draw within the city limits but isolated from the town proper. Only the roofs of two barns and a house are visible from the spot. The highway, less than half a mile away, is hidden.

The marks left by the machine are not entirely unfamiliar to experienced UFO investigators but to the two law officers they were strange. Four indentations apparently had resulted from landing gear pressing into the hard, rocky earth. At another point four circular impressions were found. The indentations were approximately three and one-half to four inches in depth, the circular impressions a little less. Almost in the middle of the area, three-quarters of a mesquite bush was charred and smoldering. The burning must have been intense and brief for weeds and earth within the area bounded by the indentations also were burned and smoking. There were no tracks.

After Zamora described his experience and what he had seen and heard, Chavez checked Zamora's car for a spade, shovel, or any implement that could have made the indentations. He found nothing. All the indentations were exactly alike.

"I just thought I'd check," Chavez said. Obviously he had found Zamora's account all but incredible.

Later questioning by Chavez and by Mr. Lorenzen and me yielded the following additional information: The color of the blue flame was an "indescribably brilliant blue." Zamora got the impression from the stance of the figures that they were "doing something to the object." His first view yielded only a long-range glance of a few seconds but he did note two protrusions that were possibly landing gear. When he stopped on the second mesa he got a good close look before the roar began and he started running. He noted landing gear or supporting elements, also some markings. The object kicked up a little dust as it rose from the ground. After it cleared the dynamite shack its ascent was at a shallow angle and it disappeared "by getting smaller" into the southwest at a high rate of speed.

After examining the landing site the two men proceeded back to headquarters in Socorro where Chavez alerted an FBI man he knew was in town. Captain Richard Holder, the Army officer in charge of the White Sands Stallion Site station, also was notified and he visited the site of the incident that same night. Rocks were piled around the indentations to preserve them, measurements and photographs were taken, and Zamora was questioned. At 7:30 the next morning, United Press International broke the story and the curious arrived to look and to trample on what little residual evidence there was.

During a lengthy discussion with Sergeant Chavez on Sunday morning, Mr. Lorenzen and I discussed our plans for analyzing the soil samples we had taken and I mentioned to Chavez that he and Zamora would probably be questioned by Air Force Intelligence. He answered that a major from Kirtland Air Force Base, near Albuquerque, and a Sergeant Moody from Wright Patterson were waiting for him down the hall. A scientist from Sandia Corporation at Albuquerque also was waiting, but after talking to Jim and me he left. From our conversation with the sergeant and the major we gathered that officialdom was very interested in the goings-on in that gully on Friday, April 24.

A very important point relating to the markings at the site of the landing is the appearance of the wedge-shaped indentations. They look as if something very heavy extended its supporting mechanism and settled to earth where its weight pushed down and consequently pushed some of the earth up and away. The bushes and grass are burned only toward the apparent center of the area.

Later during our own examination of the site we noted that shoes did make an impression on the ground but anyone wearing soft moccasins might not leave an impression.

At 2:00 p.m. on Sunday afternoon we met Patrolman Zamora. A neat man of medium height, 31 years old, he is solidly built and gives one the impression of quiet dependability. Our main concern now was with details concerning the ship or object itself, the human-shaped figures, and Zamora's reactions.

Lonnie Zamora said he thought at first an explosion had occurred and therefore he abandoned his chase of the speeding car. His observation of the two white-clad figures at the object was comparatively short and he admitted that at the time he viewed the object across the draw he thought it was an overturned car with its occupants. He did not become aware of the strange nature of the thing until he drew up onto the second mesa about 100 feet from the UFO. He still intended to investigate and did not become alarmed until flame began to shoot out of the bottom of the vehicle and the roar commenced. He thought it was going to explode and it was then he began to run.

Patrolman Zamora was reluctant to talk but I believe he told us the truth. He would not talk about the markings, however, and he intimated Captain Richard Holder, United States Army officer, had instructed him not to. We could not persuade him to describe the markings to us but managed to get a diagram from other persons to whom he had talked shortly after the incident took place. The reason for this request for silence on the subject of the markings, Captain Holder told me later, was to prepare for the possibility of corroborating evidence from other witnesses who might have seen the UFO.

Fortunately, Mr. Lorenzen and I found someone who had an accurate description of the marks which, incidentally, were not red as was later asserted by the press, but seemed to indicate the presence of an entrance hatch into the object rather than identification symbols. Judging by the apparent size of the hatch as initially described by Zamora we must assume it was convenient only for beings no more than four feet tall.

I got the definite impression that Zamora wishes the incident had not happened. He said he wished the military would tell him the object was some secret vehicle so he could forget the whole thing. He gave the further impression that he had thought it was a classified military vehicle until Captain Holder, of White Sands, announced that nothing answering the description was being tested on that range.

Zamora described the object as about the size of a car. When sketching its shape he showed the figures he had seen to be approximately one-third the length of the object itself. If the object was nine to 12 feet long, the figures were between three and four feet high.

In drawing sketches, Zamora consistently indicated legs angling outward from the bottom of the object making an angle of approximately 45 degrees with the ground plane. In making his original observation and measurements, Captain Holder noted that the appendages which made the impressions appeared to have been thrust into the ground at an angle from the direction of the general center of the quadrangle and withdrawn in the same manner.

We noted that the impressions at the point where the longest sides joined was at the lowest elevation (toward the bottom of the gulley) while the impressions marking the junction of the two shortest sides was at the highest elevation. This leads to a rather obvious solution of the irregular arrangement of the impressions. The object had rested on legs whose lengths were adjustable in order to compensate for irregular terrain while supporting the vehicle on an even keel.

Moisture content of the desert growth had been such that the fires ignited under the craft, apparently by a radiant heat source, went out by themselves. The major part of the burning took place after the vehicle had departed and ashes lay apparently undisturbed by the moderate turbulence of the takeoff.

Zamora's testimony together with the corroborating evidence on the ground furnishes some clues to the object's propulsion.

When Zamora summoned the courage to look back as he raced across the mesa he noted the brilliant blue flame, about four times as long as it was wide and extending downward from the airborne object, and saw the UFO rising slowly with a loud roaring sound. As he watched, the sound diminished, the flame subsided, and a whine, which became apparent when the roaring ceased, dropped rapidly in pitch to inaudibility. Zamora was puzzled by the lack of dust. It kicked up a little dust when it took off, but not much, he said.

Dr. J. Allen Hynek, head of the Department of Astronomy at Northwestern University, who was on the round for an Air Force–sponsored inspection, voiced the opinion that there was no evidence at the site for a thrust powerful enough to lift a vehicle of the size Zamora reported. This statement, of course, is based on our knowledge of conventional rocketry. However, we cannot dismiss Zamora's story simply because the phenomenon described is beyond the range of our technology. I believe it lies within the range of physical theory.

We are accustomed to achieve rocket lift by exhausting voluminous masses of gas, a product of combusted fuel, at relatively low acceleration. Newton's laws of reaction, however, tell us that the same effect could be achieved by exhausting a small amount of gas at considerably greater speeds. Also, if this speed approached the speed of light we might be able to take advantage of the increase in mass predicted by Einstein. The process hypothesized here could be expected to produce a high degree of ionization, the characteristic brilliant blue glow of plasma, a high level of radiant heat and, since only a small volume of matter would be ejected, turbulence might be rather minimal.

One further point: It appears that the type of power plant just described was used only to elevate the craft to a moderate altitude above the terrain. It appears that this power then was switched off in favor of some sort of "field drive." Why?

Aimé Michel's *Flying Saucers and the Straight-Line Mystery* told of landed UFOs (in France in 1954) which were reported to carry a good deal of earth with them on take-off. It was said that this soil appeared to "fall upward" leaving gaping holes in the ground. Michel theorized that a field which imparted negative weight to the UFO had done the same to the nearby earth.

Perhaps the auxiliary power, apparently used by the craft in Socorro, has been added to overcome this nuisance.

In a statement to the press on April 30, reported from Albuquerque by the Associated Press, Dr. Hynek also said he was puzzled by the lack of radar contact with these objects. He had commented several days before that the area was "infested with radar."

It is not difficult to solve the doctor's quandary.

Socorro is located just off the White Sands Proving Ground Range area. Stallion Site, which has radar, is not far from Socorro. However, the Zamora incident took place about 5:45 or 5:50 p.m. and the radar equipment at these instrumentation sites are not left on 24 hours a day. The simple answer is that the radar which pervades that part of the country was not turned on. Even if it had been, it is doubtful that radar would pick up so small an object cruising in and out of gullies, barely skimming the terrain.

Dr. Lincoln La Paz, director of the Institute of Meteoritics at the University of New Mexico, in Albuquerque, was quoted by The Albuquerque Journal as saying that "a super pogo" military craft is causing the flying saucer scare because "anyone living outside this troubled globe would be displaying absolute nonsense to come here." La Paz's statement seems a non sequitur in view of the contradictory statement by the New Mexico military commanders who said that they are testing no craft that would account for the sightings. And on May 3, Gene Kanoff, chief of administration for the National Aeronautics and Space Administration at White Sands Missile Range, said the lunar excursion module designed for the Apollo moon flight might fit Zamora's description but won't be built until later this year. Thus Dr. La Paz has given us a solution involving a nonexistent military craft.

However, it appears that the recipe for debunking again is being served up. On April 30 an Air Force "authority" publicly regretted there had been no corroborating witness and no photographs had been taken of the Zamora object.

At this writing soil samples taken at the site are in the hands of qualified and competent scientists for analysis.

I myself left Socorro convinced, for the first time in 17 years of UFO investigation, that alien beings are reconnoitering this planet.

Note: Two days after the incident, Zamora denied in a UPI story having seen any "little creatures" around the UFO. He saw only what looked like a pair of coveralls, he said.

The Lorenzens speculated that Zamora changed his story because he didn't like the implications of what he'd seen and because ridicule about "the little men" got to him. Coral Lorenzen reiterated that Patrolman Zamora did tell them, in the presence of at least three other witnesses, that he had seen two human-shaped beings in what appeared to be white "mechanic's coveralls" beside the craft.

J. Allen Hynek was at first convinced that Zamora saw some sort of secret military craft, but later realized that this could not be the case. Contrary to speculation on the part of some skeptics, Hynek did not feel that the incident was a hoax to draw tourists to the area.

UFOs Over New Guinea
By John C. Ross

March 1960

FATE's editors are extremely skeptical about "little men in flying saucers." Nevertheless, when well-documented reports are available, we feel duty-bound to report them. The following article has been prepared from a 15-page report written by the Rev. Father William Booth Gill, an Anglican Priest of the Boianai Anglican Mission of the Territory of Papua and New Guinea. It bears semi-official status, inasmuch as it was prepared at the request of R. T. Galloway, district officer of the Department of Native Affairs at Samarai. The incident was briefly reported on pages 30 and 31 of the January issue of FATE but is here presented in substantial detail.

AT 1 A.M. SUNDAY, June 21, Stephen Moi, a native teacher at Father Gill's mission, stepped outside his house and saw a bright white light coming silently out of the sky from about a quarter of a mile out to sea just west of the Boianai Station.

Four "saucermen" waved at 38 humans in one of the most sensational series of UFO sightings on record.

It descended from what seemed to be a great height and Stephen Moi watched it for about three minutes as it spiraled down eastward and parallel with the coast. The descent halted abruptly a little east of Boianai Station at a height of about 300 feet. The light remained stationary there for perhaps a half minute and gradually decreased in brilliance until the "shape of an inverted saucer" could be discerned. This shape was tilted backwards with part of its base visible. The object then moved upwards and disappeared into the clouds. Before it did so, Stephen Moi was able to make out what appeared to be four round black spots on the underside the object's base.

"When first sighted I thought it was a light similar to the flares dropped by planes during the war," Stephen Moi said.

Comment: When questioned by Father Gill, Stephen Moi denied he ever had heard of "flying saucers" before. Father Gill asked him if he was quite sure of the shape, and if the object was not more like a plate, or like a sixpence, or like a ball. Moi insisted that it was more like a saucer than anything else.

FATHER GILL was particularly interested in Stephen Moi's detailed descriptions because flying lights, strange aerial phenomena and unknown flying objects had been seen in the vicinity of Boianai Station for several months and were to continue to be seen for several more weeks after June 21.

This report and analysis is primarily concerned with the events of June 21, 26, 27, and 28, however.

The events of June 26 were far more sensational than those reported by Stephen Moi five days before. Father Gill kept a minute-by-minute log of them from 6:45 p.m. to 11:04 p.m.—four hours and 19 minutes!

Father Gill himself sighted the first object at 6:45 p.m. when from his front door he saw a bright light headed in a northwesterly direction. He called Stephen Moi and a schoolboy, Eric Kodawara, and sent Eric to round up more witnesses.

Stephen Moi said that the light was like the one he had seen five days before. It came closer, diminished in brightness, and seemed to descend to perhaps 500 feet, turning orange or a deep orangey-yellow.

At 6:55 p.m. a "figure" appeared on top of the saucer-shaped object. It moved. Shortly three "figures" were visible atop the object, which Father Gill now refers to as a "deck." They moved and they glowed. A few minutes later they were gone again and by 7:10 p.m. there were four of them. Then the "figures" disappeared from the "deck" and a blue spotlight appeared, shining upwards. Two minutes later, two "figures" were back. At 7:20 p.m. the spotlight went off and the "figures" were gone. Just then the UFO went through a cloud. It was not seen again until 8:28 p.m.

At this time there was clear sky overhead but heavy clouds over Dogura. Father Gill called the residents of the Station together again to watch the UFO with him. The object appeared to descend and it seemed nearer than before—or nearer than the previous object had been—but it did not seem to be so large. Then a second object was seen over the ocean, hovering at times, and at 8:35 p.m. another was sighted over Wadobuna Village, only a mile or so away.

At about 8:50 p.m. a large UFO was seen. It was stationary, and Father Gill asks in his notes, "Was it the original one?" Other smaller ones were coming and going through patchy clouds, which were beginning to form again. As they bored through the clouds they reflected lights onto the clouds like large halos. Father Gill estimated the level of the cloud base at "2,000 feet, probably less." By this time, Father Gill was thinking of the large UFO as a "Mother Ship" and the smaller ones as "Satellites."

By 9:05 p.m. three of the four Satellites had gone but the "Mother Ship" remained large, clear and stationary for five minutes; then it left, giving out a red light. The last Satellite now left or disappeared into a cloud. At 9:20 p.m. the Mother Ship reappeared, headed out across the sea towards Giwa, at high speed, its color changing from thin white to deep red and then to blue-green. It was gone by 9:30 p.m.

At 9:46 p.m. another UFO appeared overhead, hovering. It remained there for about 25 minutes, and at 10:10 either went behind a cloud or was covered by a cloud. At 10:30 it was seen very high, hovering in a clear patch of sky between clouds.

This was the last visual sighting of the evening. The sky became overcast at 10:50 p.m. and at 11:04 p.m. there was heavy rain.

Because of the presence of nearby mountains, and the fact that the UFOs were often below the clouds and their glow reflected on the underside of the clouds, which covered known heights on the mountains, Father Gill concluded that the UFOs descended to below 2,000 feet and that the first sighting, over the sea, seemed not more than 500 feet above the water at times.

Altogether there were 38 witnesses of this sighting, 27 of whose names we have on file since they attest to the facts above.

Another interesting fact is that the first Satellite to appear this night had five panels of bright "windows" or "portholes" visible at its edge. They seemed to be like alternate vertical bands of light from top to bottom of the UFO.

Comment: We shall reserve detailed comment on this sighting to the end, but we would like to apologize to Father Gill here for using the word "figures" to designate the beings that appeared to be moving about the "deck" of the "Mother Ship." The words "deck" and "Mother Ship" are Father Gill's. The word "figures" is our own. Father Gill called them "men."

THE NEXT NIGHT at 6 p.m., Saturday, June 27, a native named Annie Laurie saw a large UFO in about the same position as the previous night's first sighting. Father Gill saw it at 6:02 p.m. and called several other people from the Station. The sun had set but it was still quite light and remained so for about 15 more minutes.

"We watched figures appear on top—four of them—no doubt that they were human," Father Gill writes. "Possibly the same object that I took to be the Mother Ship last night. Two smaller UFOs were seen at the same time, stationary. One above the hills west, another overhead.

"On the large one, two of the figures seemed to be doing something near the center of the deck—were occasionally bending over and raising their arms as though adjusting or 'setting up' something (not visible).

"One figure seemed to be standing looking down at us (a group of about a dozen). I stretched my arm above my head and waved. To our surprise the figure did the same. Ananias (a native teacher) waved both arms over his head and then the two outside figures did the same. Ananias and myself began waving our arms and all four now seemed to wave back. There seemed to be no doubt that our movements were answered. All mission boys made audible gasps (of either joy or surprise, perhaps both)."

"As dark was beginning to close in, I sent Eric Kodawara for a torch and directed a series of long dashes toward the UFO. After a minute or two of this, the UFO apparently acknowledged by making several wavering motions back and forth. Waving by us was repeated and this followed by more flashes of torch, then the UFO began slowly to become bigger, apparently coming in our direction.

"It ceased after perhaps half a minute and came on no further. After an additional two or three minutes, the figures apparently lost interest in us for they disappeared 'below' deck. At 6:25 p.m. two figures reappeared to carry on with whatever they were doing before the interruption. The blue spotlight came on for a few seconds, twice in succession."

While all this was going on the two other UFOs remained stationary—apparently higher than the previous evening because they appeared smaller. At 6:30 p.m. Father Gill went in to dinner. At 7:00 p.m. the first UFO was still present but appeared smaller. The observers went to church for Evensong. When Evensong was over at 7:45 p.m. the sky was overcast and visibility poor.

Nothing more was seen that night but about 10:40 p.m. there was a loud explosion just outside the Mission House. About 25 minutes later there were a few drops of rain. Father Gill suggested that the explosion may have been a thunderclap but if so it was not an ordinary explosion. It seemed to be just outside the window and was a "penetrating, earsplitting explosion." It waked people on the station.

Comment: How soon a thing may become old hat. Here it was only the third day of important sightings and Father Gill did not choose to delay dinner over them. The routine of the Station already was almost back to normal.

THE NEXT DAY was Sunday but UFOs apparently do not observe the Sabbath-at least the Sabbath of No. 3 Planet out from Sol. The first UFO appeared nearly overhead at 6:45 p.m. It was very high, hovering, but still distinguishable. Forty-five minutes later it had moved to a southern position but was still more or less overhead. At 9:00 p.m. three UFOs were sighted high, proceeding almost in a straight line. The sky was clear.

At 11 p.m. eight UFOs appeared—the greatest number yet seen at one time. One was fairly low, but except for occasional hovering, no activity was visible on board.

At 11:20 p.m. there was a sharp metallic bang on the Mission House roof, as though a piece of metal had dropped on it from a great height. There was no roll of an object down the roof slope afterwards. Nothing could be found, but four UFOs were circling round the station at the time. All were high. Father Gill went to bed at 11:30 p.m. The UFOs were still present.

Next morning the roof was examined, but there was no apparent mark or dent where anything had struck it.

It may be that Father Gill regretted going to bed at his usual time that night because there were no further sightings at the time.

On July 6 around 8:40 p.m. however, the Reverend David Durie, acting principal of St. Aidon's College in nearby Dogura, noticed a white glow similar to that caused by the moon, through a cloud cover. As he watched, the glow changed to a brilliant spot of white light, descending and moving a little to the south. This gradually faded, then after five minutes it glowed again brilliantly, seemed to turn in a circular motion, counterclockwise.

The glow moved further south and finally was obscured by a point of land around 9:00 p.m. Seen through his binoculars, the center of the glow appeared to be orange and shaped like a disk, Reverend Durie reported. Other witnesses included Mrs. Durie, Reverend E. Dams, Father Gill, and more than 10 other men.

On July 8 and 9 different native teachers in the vicinity saw beams of brilliant white light shining across the sea near the shore and parallel with the beach. The lights may have come from a boat but this could not be checked.

Final comments and analysis: What are we to make of this extraordinary report prepared by Father Gill?

Let us ignore, for a moment, that one of the native witnesses was a teacher named Ananias—a kind of missionary joke, apparently (other witnesses included Love Daisy Kolauna, Annie Laurie Borewa—both of them medical assistants—Kipling Guveropa, etc.).

Father Gill himself suggests alternate explanations. By July 14 he was hesitating to express definite opinions of what he might have seen—except that as far as the existence of UFOs per se is concerned, his mind had completely changed from skepticism "to the conviction that the UFOs as observed by me cannot be explained away in terms of natural phenomena."

Nonetheless, Father Gill is an honest man and he suggests he may have been mistaken because of:

1. Hallucination. In which case the 27 eyewitnesses who signed their approval of his description may also have been hallucinated.
2. Witnesses were under "suggestion," to report what they did report. Father Gill remarks that the inexperienced natives may have been under undue influence from the more sophisticated Europeans. Or they may have agreed with them because of a subservient attitude.

We think this is a sound point. We do not state unequivocally that the particular New Guinea personality involved in these sightings may be more susceptible to suggestion or subservience but it's likely to be. We suggest, too, that in his role of priest Father Gill would predispose these natives to equating him with "medicine man" and therefore worker of magic. The UFOs obviously would qualify in this area.

3. Illusion. Father Gill suggests that "freak" atmospheric conditions or subjectiveness on the part of observers might have resulted in a misinterpretation of natural phenomena.

We think this applies to many of the details of his description but not to the overall validity of the details. Note especially in this connection that human beings, including the watchers on the beach, tend to interpret what they see in terms of that with which they are familiar.

In this manner, moving figures or objects aboard the UFOs become "men," the top of the UFO becomes a "deck," the large object becomes a "Mother Ship" (totally without evidence), the smaller objects become "satellites," the figures "wave" to them, and so on. All these are loaded words and their use probably is not justified by Father Gill.

Assume, for example, that Father Gill actually did see figures moving aboard the "deck" of the UFO. It was night; they were probably at least a quarter of a mile away and a minimum of 400 feet in the air; and they were illuminated only by a glow. But the human mind, knowing that on a man-made vehicle such moving objects would be certain to be men, invariably interprets the figures as men. For all of that, they could have been moving pieces of machinery. Or other kinds of animals. Or something else...

Another case in point will be noted on the accompanying drawing. The UFOs appear to have four straight legs pointing diagonally downward from their base. A number of observers believed they saw such "legs." Stephen Moi, however, who saw the first UFO on June 21, was able to make out only four round black spots on the underside of the object. The human mind naturally makes a jump under such circumstances and adds the "legs" which may not have been there at all.

4. Unreliable observers. Father Gill suggests that the objects may have been some kind of astronomical phenomena and were reported as UFOs because the observers were not familiar with such phenomena.

We know of no such phenomena ourselves, and we know of no astronomers who do.

5. Reliability of witnesses. This is a somewhat different matter than Point 4. The only question here is: are the witnesses honest men?

Immediately after the sightings of June 26, Father Gill brought 38 witnesses together into a well-lighted room. Three of the observers, going to separate parts of the room, made sketches of what they believed they had seen. When compared, the sketches essentially varied only in size.

Twenty-seven of the 38 observers attested to the accuracy of the three drawings and that they had seen objects that corresponded to them.

But what of the 11 witnesses who did not sign? Were they also honest men?

In the aggregate, we are inclined to be open-minded on the testimony of the natives—even the native teachers, on the grounds that they might be overly anxious to please.

So we come down eventually to the credibility of the white observers present, and especially of Father Gill himself.

Even discounting a great deal of what Father Gill believes he saw, he still has reported one of the most significant series of sightings on record. Unless, of course, there was more than one Ananias in the New Guinea record.

I Photographed Space Ships
By Prof. George Adamski

July 1951

I saw a spaceship for the first time on the night of October 9, 1946, during a meteoric shower created by the Giacobini-Zinner Comet. As those who were interested in the display will recall, its brilliance was diminished because of the light of the moon. A dozen or so persons had come up to Palomar Gardens to spend the evening in the mountains where they could watch the shower without interference of city lights.

All of these people, as well as those of us who make our home at the Gardens, were outside watching this heavenly display when suddenly a gigantic, dark dirigible-type object appeared low over the mountains to the south of us, where it seemed to hover for several minutes. The contrast between the dark body and the light of the night enabled us to observe it carefully. One notable difference between this ship and a modern dirigible was its streamlined form.

There was no exterior cabin of any kind. It appeared as a huge cigar-shaped object hovering in the sky without visible lights of any kind.

I had seen the *Graf Zeppelin* in its day and many other such craft, similar in shape but smaller in size, but this one we were now watching was much the largest I had ever seen and I wondered where it had come from since I had not heard of our government having any such airships in use at this time.

After a few minutes its nose raised to what appeared to be about a 45 degree angle from the position in which it had been hovering and it shot up and away at a speed that seemed impossible for such a huge craft to move, leaving an orange trail that remained in the air for several minutes.

The people who had come up to watch the meteoric shower asked me what that object was.

I told them I didn't know.

When finally we went indoors, I turned on the radio and tuned in KFSD, San Diego, for a news report. We were all amazed to hear the announcer telling of an immense space ship which hundreds of people in San Diego and for many miles up the coast had seen while they were watching the shower. So great was the interest of some of the people there that they had prevailed upon a well-known spiritualist medium to attempt to project her mind out into outer space, follow the ship, and find out who they were and why they had not landed on earth when they had been so close.

Articles about this ship also appeared the next day in the San Diego papers and the *Los Angeles Daily News*.

Later the medium's report was given over the radio. She was reported to have said that this ship had come from one of the other planets in our system; that its occupants had not landed on earth because they were not sure how they would be received by earthmen. The name of the planet was not given.

Almost a year later, in August 1947, about 9:30 p.m., I was sitting in the yard swing watching the heavens. As I watched, a bright ball of light appeared from behind a mountain peak to the east and sped across the sky toward the west as if shot from some gigantic cannon far off in the distance. I heard no sound. Then a second ball of light followed the path of the first. Then another and another and I wondered what they were.

I strolled across the gardens to see how far I could watch them in their course. They had kept coming but I had not thought to count them, so busy was I wondering what these strange things were. Since some of our government experimental grounds are many miles to the east of Palomar, I though these might be some new experimental devices being shot through the air in tests. But when one of these big balls of light stopped in its path and actually backed up, I knew I was viewing something from out of this world.

I called my wife and the three women who operate the café to come out to see what was happening. They brought with them two pairs of binoculars and I went to my telescope in order to observe these objects more clearly.

We counted 184 after then and it seemed that every 32nd one would cross above the mountain chain until, just before it left our line of vision, it would reverse its path, sometimes almost all the way back toward the east to the point of its first appearance. There it would stop completely, hover a full second or more, and then move forward again to disappear from behind the mountains in the southwest. Then would follow another 31 brilliant balls of light, one at a time but all traveling the same invisible path through the sky.

If we had been watching them from a higher vantage point, they probably would have appeared as a very long chain, much as Kenneth Arnold described the nine he had seen in June of the same year "flying past Mt. Ranier." At that time, none of us had heard of Arnold and his experience.

One feature we were all able to observe distinctly was that each of these objects had the appearance of the planet Saturn—that is, each looked like a large ball encircled by a ring which appeared to be separate from the ball itself. This was discernible both as the objects passed directly before us and also as many of them banked before shooting off toward the ocean and out of sight. Nor was it necessary to use either the binoculars or the telescope to note these particular features.

While these instruments did bring the objects into closer and sharper view, their speed of movement was so fast that some of the women preferred watching with their naked eyes. I believe this parade was of space ships, which we now choose to call "saucers," and it lasted for about an hour and a half. They shot before us in single file and seldom were there two in view at the same time. The last one passed across the sky, banked as if to go toward the ocean, stopped completely, reversed halfway back the path it had just covered, stopped directly over one of the highest peaks to the south, and from there shot out four intensely bright beams of light, two toward Palomar and two in the opposite direction toward San Diego. These were left on for perhaps 15 seconds. When they were turned off and the ship sped out of sight in the west.

The next morning a soil-conservation man, Tony Delmonte, with whom I had often discussed space ships and the probability of life on other planets but who still remained a skeptic, came in and asked me if I had seen any space ships the night before.

I asked him if he was kidding or what he had reference to.

He replied that this time he was frankly serious and was ready to admit space ships were real for he had seen them himself. He said that the evening before, with a group of ranchers from Pauma Valley, he was at Demsey's Ranch in the valley. Since the evening was warm these men were all sitting outdoors when they saw the first of these objects shoot across the sky, then another and another. They, too, wondered what in the world they were for they were too large for meteors and their movement through space was not in accordance with any object dropping from out of space toward the earth. They wondered if this were some new type of light beam being projected into the sky for tests. But the shape wasn't right for that and there was no connecting beam between the moving portion and the sending instrument, as is normal; nor were any clouds visible in the sky upon which to reflect such a light if an invisible light beam had been developed. Then they saw the first object stop in air, remain motionless for a second, and then move in reverse.

This must have been the one I first noticed, for they had started counting with the first ship they had noticed and counted 204 while I had started counting with this ship and had counted 184.

The same morning a group of scientists stopped in and asked me if I had seen anything unusual in the sky the night before.

I told them what I had seen and what Mr. Delmonte had told me.

They asked me if I had counted the number I had seen pass; if so, how many.

I gave them the two different totals and they indicated the larger number was more nearly correct. This was before the big mirror had been brought up to Mount Palomar.

So firm was my conviction of the reality of space ships and visitors from other planets that I stated this fact to those guests of the Gardens who questioned me on the subject. We had many long and interesting discussions along the lines of their reality, their purpose, the motivating power used, and the probable types of people who could develop such spacecraft.

I found people for the most part were interested but few had seen them, many feared them and a large proportion were frankly skeptical. So I decided to prove my point, if possible, with photographs. I could have taken some very good pictures of this parade of "saucers" if I had had any film; but I had none at that time. Not until a year and a half later, in February 1949, was I successful in getting my first picture of space ships. This is the one that was published in the September 1950 issue of FATE.

In October 1949, I was guest speaker for the Fallbrook, California, Rotary Club where I talked about the reality of space ships. This was the first of many similar lectures before service clubs in Southern California, which continued through the year of 1950. I did this in spite of official denials and ridicule from some of my acquaintances in the fields of science.

As time has passed I have found more and more people who have found more and more people who have observed strange objects moving through the sky—people who I have good reason to believe are not subject to hallucinations.

From time to time, with the aid of my 6-inch telescope, a Newtonian with a 54-inch focal length, made by the Tinsley's Laboratory in Berkeley, California, I have attempted to photograph what I saw moving at such a terrific speed and so far out from our earth. To do this, I attached a Hagee-Dresden, Graflex Type box camera, which I had converted especially for this purpose, over the eyepiece of the telescope, thereby using it in place of the lens of the camera. The shutter speed is 100.

This camera has holders for cut film, which I use instead of plates or roll film. Since all objects that I have observed have been moving through space at terrific speeds, I obtain the fastest possible film for this work. My pictures were taken on Eastman Super Panchro Press-Sports Type film cut to size 2½ inches by 3½ inches to fit the holder of the camera.

Once the camera is adjusted and focused to the ground glass in the back, the holder with the film is then put in, ready to shoot, while steady observation is maintained through the finder on the telescope.

The percentage of success in this field is very low, depending more on luck than accuracy—but I have succeeded in getting some very good snapshots.

Of course during the extended length of time I have been observing the heavens in search of ships from outer space, I have seen both large space ships and those objects which we term "saucers" during the daytime as well as during the night. However, due to the brightness of the daytime sun, such objects are very difficult to photograph during the day and I have made no effort to do so.

I have taken all my pictures at night by the light of the moon because often I had noticed that a good number of the ships I saw moving through space appeared headed for the moon. Some of them seemed to land on the moon, close to the rim; while others passed over the rim and disappeared behind it.

Startling as it may seem, I believe the moon has an atmosphere. I have observed through my telescopes for the past 18 years. At one time or another I have seen meteorites falling on the moon. One cannot see a meteor falling on the moon unless it is burning, thereby showing up in contrast to the light of the moon. To do this, some sort of atmosphere must be present or a meteor would not burn there any more than it burns in outer space. Those which we see coming toward our earth burn only after they enter our atmosphere.

In view of what I have observed through my telescopes, I figure it is logical to believe that space ships might be using our moon for a base in their interplanetary travels; just as we are planning to use it for our first stop when we venture out toward Mars or Venus or any other planet in space.

On the other hand, if we were traveling toward a planet we know to be inhabited yet where we weren't too sure of how we would be received, what would be our method of procedure? I reasoned that if we could land safely on one of that planet's satellites within 200,000 or 300,000 miles of our destination, we would first establish a base, unload whatever supplies we had, and from this base we would venture forth toward the planet on frequent sorties (missions) for close observation of the planet, its people and what was going on there, with the idea of future landing.

Whether my analysis is right or wrong I do not know, but the pictures which I have succeeded in getting seem to indicate that such might be the case.

Most of these ships have been caught with the moon as a background, or as they were nearing the moon. My reason for doing this was to have some known body in space, whose distance from the earth is known, by which distances of the ships or saucers might be judged to some degree. The moon has served this purpose.

Watching through my telescope during the early morning hours of May 6, 1950, I observed a bright object moving at terrific speed through space and it seemed to me it was heading straight for the moon. I had my camera set, so I quickly took three shots in the hope of catching it in one. I marked the plates in order as I removed each from the camera. Not being able to estimate its speed accurately, it was impossible to set the camera and be sure of anything. It was more lucky guessing than accurate figuring. On the other hand, I had been watching constantly for well over an hour before this ship suddenly flashed across my vision. From there on it was fast action and good luck.

There is a certain amount of reflection from the moon in the first picture. The second one shows more light reflected while the third picture is brightest of all, indicating the rising of the sun at that early hour even though the sun was yet below the horizon from my point of observation.

But the most outstanding thing about this picture is the shadow the big ship is casting on the moon. To those trained in aerial photography, the shadow is instantly discernible. Yet I had had these pictures for several months, had shown them to many people and did not realize the shadow was showing in this picture until it was shown to me, for I have not had such training.

Early in November 1950, having heard much of me and my pictures, a group of high ranking military men whose names and branches of service I cannot give since they are all still in active service, came to my place to see my pictures and to question me concerning them; also to look through my telescopes. All of these men have been well trained in aerial photography and in reading aerial photographs. When I handed them an enlargement of this picture, one of them remarked, "Why that object is casting its shadow upon the moon."

All the others verified this statement and between themselves, using the shadow as one factor, they began estimating the size of the ship and its possible distance from the moon.

They did not give me their figures but reminded me that any object moving through space must be relatively close to the earth to cast its shadow upon the earth and this would also be true of any object casing its shadow upon the moon. Figuring the size of the shadow and considering the fact that it was made by an object moving at very high speed, they said that if the ship could be photographed without reflection it actually would be only a small fraction of the size shown in this picture, due to the reflected brilliance.

All the men were intensely interested in this picture especially, and after looking through my telescope, both at the moon and at Jupiter, which at that time was also visible in the evening sky, they said they understood how I could have taken the picture I have. Apparently they had come up to make sure for themselves that I really have what I claim to have. They had come as skeptics; they left fully convinced, not by my words but by what they had seen for themselves.

The reason for the luminosity of this ship and all those in the other pictures is that being made of metal or some metallic substance, they reflect the sunlight with more intensity than does the moon.

The moon, being of earthy substance, has a tendency to absorb a certain amount of sunlight and reflects only a portion of that which hits it, while a metal body reflects practically the entire amount of light hitting it. Any object in space, whether it is a ship, a moon, or a planet, if it is out far enough to be in direct line with the sun's rays will reflect light from those rays in direct proportion to its own qualities of absorption and reflection.

Intense reflections as given off by the ship in this picture are somewhat unfortunate, since it makes it next to impossible to obtain definite markings, which are undoubtedly on all interplanetary ships, the same as they are on earth ships. But one thing is certain—there is definitely some solid body moving through space far out beyond the earth's atmosphere and it is reflecting the sun's light. And since I doubt sincerely that our government or any other nation on earth had craft capable of going so close to the moon as to cast a shadow upon it, these craft must be coming from some other planet or some other system.

The ship in one of my photos, I believe, is the type that Captain Thomas. F. Mantell was chasing when he was killed. (Mantell's crash on January 7, 1948, while piloting an F-51 over Mansville, Kentucky, is often considered the first death attributed to a UFO.) According to printed records, he reported that the ship he was trying to catch was a monster, without wings. This one is of that type; showing definitely its reflected outline, while the tail part is irregular; possibly caused by the vapor from the type of propulsion it uses.

It is a recognized fact that ships traveling through space, as theses ships do, encounter meteors and dust particles which are found everywhere in space. These would destroy any ship unless it had a magnetic repulsing force extending quite a distance into space from its body. Of course this force is invisible, even though very powerful. It is possible that Captain Mantell was hit by this repelling force, which disintegrated his airplane.

I am not copying this magnetic force idea from Frank Scully's book, for my own book, *Pioneers of Space*, was published and on the market months before the factual information given by Mr. Scully was even completed in manuscript form. In my book I mention such a force as a possibility for interplanetary ships.

Other pictures were taken during the early portion of the nights of May 27 and May 29, 1950. The reflections of the bodies in these pictures are round instead of long. This naturally gives them the appearance of being those objects we have named "saucers." There is a definite contrast of their reflections to that of the moon.

In one of these pictures can be seen seven saucers in what appears to be a formation. I had been observing the moon closely for more than an hour and had noted a number of small bright spots on the moon, almost like lights flashing or water reflecting, but it was not until they started moving that I was sure in my own mind what I had been watching. As the first of these objects moved across the rim of the moon I snapped the shutter of the camera attached to my telescope and this picture is the result.

The optics of my telescope bring the moon to within 100 miles of the earth, so the possibility of such pictures as I have succeeded in obtaining is more easily understandable to those who have never looked through a telescope and think only of the moon as being approximately 240,000 miles distant from the earth.

Another picture shows four saucers in almost square formation, not too far away from the crater edge of the moon's photograph. In this case, the moon was much more exposed than in the previous pictures. These saucers appeared to come from behind the moon since they had not been visible on the face of the moon nor had I observed them in space moving toward the moon before they came into view in my telescope finder. I snapped this picture and then continued watching the saucers as they moved through space away from the moon.

The third of these pictures was half exposed to light and I caught only a portion of the moon in this one, but there are definitely two saucers in this photograph—one at the edge of the moon while another is following the first toward the moon. These I observed far out in space as I was scanning the heavens with my naked eyes. As I noted them flashing across the sky apparently toward the moon, I succeeded in getting them in my finder and caught the picture.

The last of these pictures, showing two very luminous balls of light with trails and two smaller objects which appear to be farther out in space, was not taken with the moon in the background because they were not in line with the moon when they flashed through space and I succeeded in getting a shot of them. The two larger ones were within the earth's atmosphere—I would say probably out about 75 to 100 miles from earth. All four of these I saw with my naked eyes before catching them in the finder of the telescope and succeeding in photographing them. But this same picture with the illumination of the two larger objects cut down completely blacks out the two smaller ones that are obviously much farther out in space. They definitely show the outlines of the saucers. Such objects have been well described by trained observers on several occasions during the past three years.

Taking such pictures as these requires much time and patience. They are not easy to catch, nor are there ships or saucers always moving through space to be caught in photographs. There have been times when I observed regularly through my telescopes for a month and didn't see any such objects moving through space. Then again I have seen several of them during a single night. That is the way I have worked in getting the pictures I have. Of over 200 shots, I have 11 good pictures. But I shall continue my efforts to get better ones for I feel sure this can be done.

During the evening of October 14, 1950, some friends came up to look through my telescopes. While we were looking at Pleiades, two ships crossed the path of our vision at a terrific speed. We all saw them, for they were visible with the naked eye. These friends had never before seen anything like space ships and while they had talked with me several times about such things, they still wondered. When they saw those ships flash past, their excitement knew no bounds. Their enthusiasm is now sincere and they are firmly convinced that there are space ships moving through space. Had I had my equipment ready for shooting, I could have got a good picture of these ships.

Meeting with the Martian
By Aimé Michel

September 1957

The center of France has some spots that are among the wildest and most backward in Europe. The peasants and sheepherders of these areas are known for their austerity and faithful clinging to customs and morals—some of which date back to the time of the Celts, that is to say, over 20 centuries. One would not expect to find among these people minds obsessed with science fiction.

However, it is in one of these very sectors that, for the first time in Europe, a man claims to have seen and even touched with his hand a being from outer space. The affair took place September 10, 1954, at nightfall, three days after the sighting at Contay [see FATE, July 1957].

It was 8:30 p.m. when Antoine Mazaud returned to his farm. "Are you sick?" his wife asked him. "You seem pale, and your hands are trembling. What happened?"

Madame Mazaud had good reason to be concerned. Her husband, a solid man in his 50s, was a stable peasant, as sensible as he was robust.

"No," he answered. "I'm fine. But I had a bizarre experience—really an inexplicable meeting."

His wife asked, "Who did you meet?"

"Who? You would better ask, what. I'll tell you. But I forbid you to tell anyone. I don't want any trouble."

And Mr. Mazaud told this story:

He had worked all afternoon in his oat field. Around 8:30, night was falling and he decided to return home. Throwing his pitchfork onto his shoulder he took the path leading from the hamlet of Mourieras to his home, about 1,500 meters away. This path twists between two hedgerows in a wild, hilly countryside.

While walking through a small wood he put down his pitchfork in order to roll a cigarette. (I add this small detail so that the American reader will understand the character of this person and this place—far removed from the novels of H. G. Wells.) This task took him a minute or two, after which he put his pitchfork back on his shoulder and started out again.

"I had taken only a few steps," he said, "when in the beginning darkness I found myself face to face with a strange being dressed in a peculiar way. He was of medium height and was wearing a sort of helmet, without earpieces, somewhat like a motorcycle helmet.

"My first thought was to defend myself with my pitchfork," he said. "I was scared stiff. The other also was immobilized. Then, very slowly, he came towards me, making a gesture above his head with an arm. I think he wanted to calm me, perhaps to greet me or to express his friendship. His other arm was extended to me but not in a menacing manner.

"I didn't know what to do. After a moment of panic, during which I was asking myself with whom and what I was dealing, I thought perhaps it was an insane person who had disguised himself. As he continued to come slowly towards me, making strange gestures like salaams, I decided that he didn't intend to attack me.

"He was in front of me. Then, as I still was holding my pitchfork in my right hand, I offered him my left, hesitatingly.

He took it, shook it very hard and then, brusquely, held me to him, pulling my head against his helmet. All this took place in complete silence.

"I was recovering from my stupor. I took courage and spoke to him. He did not answer, but passed in front of me and went a couple of yards away into the heavy shadows of the woods. It seemed to me then that he kneeled. A few seconds later I heard a kind of buzzing whistle and saw rising, almost vertically, towards the sky between the branches a sort of dark machine. It seemed to be shaped like a cigar puffed out on one side and about three or four yards long. It passed under the high-tension wires and disappeared to the west, in the direction of Limoges.

"It was only at this moment that my reason returned," continued Mr. Mazaud. "I ran in the direction he had disappeared but obviously it was too late."

Truth requires me to add that while telling his tale, both to the police and later to the press, Mr. Mazaud always said he regretted not having held his strange visitor by force and even "that I did not kill him with my pitchfork in order to know what it was." One must remember that this peasant did not feel that he had been in the presence of a real man.

After Mr. Mazaud told his wife this story that night of September 10, 1954, he again cautioned her to repeat it to no one. "They would laugh at us," he said.

So naturally Madame Mazaud told her neighbor in strictest secrecy. And she, in turn, repeated it to the travelling salesman, who reported it to the police.

The investigation by the lieutenant of police of Ossel started on the 12th, two days later. Antoine Mazaud, in a very bad mood, had to be begged to talk.

The police went to the scene of the "meeting," examined the underbrush but found nothing suspicious. Two days had passed since the supposed meeting, and it had rained heavily.

Since there was only one witness, the police at first took the most reasonable view of the thing—that of an hallucination or a joke. They could find nothing to prove the peasant's story, but at the same time Mr. Mazaud had an excellent reputation around the countryside. He was a hard-working man, taciturn, well-balanced, and without imagination. The impression made on the police, the investigators, the journalists, by the man was the same. Here is how the correspondent from Combat, the intellectual paper of Paris, describes him:

"There is about his account an indisputable aura of sincerity. The investigators were not able to uncover the least fault or contradiction in his statements."

The Commissioner of General Information at Tulle (a position similar to lieutenant or captain with the FBI) was surprised, as was everyone, by the serious nature of the man who had been the unwilling witness of this strange being.

Lastly, it is important to mention that, until the arrival of the journalists, Mr. Mazaud had not thought of connecting his experience with stories of flying saucers, words which meant nothing to him during the first days following his observation. Now, however, he refers to his mysterious visitor as "this Martian."

The Bureau of General Information and the police would have placed his adventure in the category of daydreams—and I would never have mentioned it—except for one small detail.

The last words of his story were, "the object passed under the high tension wires and disappeared in the sky to the west, in the direction of Limoges."

While conducting their investigation, the police discovered that on the night of September 10, a few seconds after 8:30, the inhabitants of Limoges saw in the sky a reddish disc that discharged a bluish trail. It was flying from east to west. The reports of these witnesses were taken before the incident at Mourieras was known to anyone (the first newspaper articles are dated September 14). Among the witnesses is Mr. Georges Frugier, 30 years old, who reported his observation of the night of September 10. One cannot help noticing that the reports completely authenticate each other.

Mr. Mazaud said 8:30.

Mr. Frugier said a few minutes after 8:30.

The object disappeared to the west in the direction of Limoges, said Mr. Mazaud.

The disc arrived from the east and disappeared towards the west, say the witnesses at Limoges.

Finally, it is remarkable that in the case of Mr. Frugier, his own family started to take his story seriously only after reading in the papers of September 14th about the incident at Mourieras.

You may choose any one of the following conclusions:

1. Mr. Mazaud saw nothing at all—he invents Science Fiction novels in his Limoges colloquialisms while he rolls his own cigarettes.
2. Or he had a hallucination.
3. Or he saw a helicopter (we know about the agility of this aircraft and how it can slide between the leaves of the underbrush) and its pilot (whose passion is to kiss old peasants at nightfall).
4. And that at the same time the inhabitants of Limoges saw nothing at all and by telepathy completed Mr. Mazaud's novel or else saw a slow-falling star called up by the reverie of the old peasant—or vice versa.
5. Or you may conclude Mr. Mazaud and the citizens of Limoges saw a flying saucer.

If you find any of the first four conclusions reassuring let me ask you, just how far can you legitimately carry its applications? This is what the amateur explainers must once and for all decide. No doubt one could prove that Generals Lee and Grant were really only badly interpreted phenomena. But how would the soldiers at Gettysburg have felt about this?

[Editor's Note: For what it's worth, Grant was not at Gettysburg. At the time, he was winding up the siege of Vicksburg, Mississippi.]

ETs, Phone Here
By Scott Nicholson

June 1999

Where does an outsider turn for help in a human world? A woman who exists simultaneously in two sets of dimensions is willing to lend a sympathetic ear.

Lori Cordini says she's a dual person. By this she means that she lives both a three-dimensional human life and a four-dimensional existence as a "light being." She's on a mission to come to terms with that duality as well as help others understand their own dual existences.

Cordini's first brush with the other world was as a child. She remembers a white light that "lit up the sky like it was noon."

"That incident has stuck with me all my life," she says. "I have often wondered what really happened. Every time I asked my mother, she'd say it was a meteorite that landed in New Mexico and Arizona, and that would be the end of it."

It happened in July 1947, the month of the crash in Roswell, New Mexico.

Almost 50 years later, in 1995, Cordini became obsessed with learning what had really happened. Though not particularly interested in UFOs, she went to a Mutual UFO Network meeting near her home in the Blue Ridge Mountains of North Carolina. A woman there described being abducted by aliens. The woman's use of the word "lonely" in her account struck an emotional chord with Cordini, who underwent hypnosis in the ensuing weeks.

"As the hypnotist put me in a trance, I remembered the whole incident," Cordini says. "A beam of light came through the house, I was pulled through the wall, and my mother grabbed my feet. My mother was very relaxed, but I could sense that she felt frustrated because she couldn't help."

After the session, Cordini called her mother and again asked about the incident. This time, her mother told the same story that Cordini had just remembered under hypnosis.

"She spoke with a knowledge of the cosmos and the universe that I can't explain," Cordini says. "The thought that kept going through my mind was, 'This is Mom? She has an eighth-grade education. How does she know about UFOs? How does she know that I don't belong to this Earth?'"

Under hypnosis, Cordini also remembered contact with an extraterrestrial species, a childhood encounter with what she calls "Mr. Pumpkin Man." Cordini recalls an alien in a space suit hanging outside her window. The creature sent her a telepathic message that it was dying. She was frustrated because she was a child and didn't know how to help it.

A third recovered memory involves an airplane hangar and military personnel. This is a puzzle to which Cordini is still collecting the pieces. "I was on a mother ship, working," she says. "Because of time travel, we were taken onboard to do our work there and brought back to a time before we left so we didn't have any gaps.

"I was being brought back to Earth with three extraterrestrials," she says. "We were in what I call a pod. We were either shot down or we crashed near Edwards Air Force Base. I was standing around the crash site, dazed, seeing the dead bodies. I was handcuffed, thrown in the back seat of a limousine, and taken away. That's when the interrogation began.

"I found myself lying on a cold metal table, and I thought, *This is a standard abduction thing*. There were military people around me, plus [another member of] that interesting little species from my childhood, though this one was wearing a blue jogging suit."

Through telepathy, Cordini learned that the alien was pleased to be helping the government officials, but that military personnel were taking advantage of the alien's trust.

"If someone asked me which was I afraid of, humans or ETs, I'd definitely say humans," she says. "ETs are nothing. They're loving, they're kind, they're caring, they're supportive. Humans are vicious animals. Not as a whole, of course," she adds.

Dial M for Multidimensionality

Cordini believes that her role is to help humans prepare for imminent changes. "We're part of the vanguard," she says. "We're here to assist humans during the transition. My job here on Earth is to open up people's awareness—not only their own self-awareness, but their intergalactic awareness."

After her own flashbacks, Cordini set up a telephone support line for people who have encountered phenomena beyond easy explanation. With help from her husband, Carl, she started the Intergalactic Contact Center to share and collect the experiences of others.

"It's not about little green men," Cordini says. "It's about who we are as human beings and where we come from, our relationship to the cosmos, how the Earth got here, how we're interrelated, and the endless, endless journey."

Humans must take responsibility for their actions, according to Cordini. "The time has come to examine our belief systems, to examine our history … and make decisions for ourselves," she says. "Look at death, look at life, look at our relationship to the cosmos. We're all sentient beings. We all have duality, meaning we have a body and a soul. Soul lives forever, body doesn't."

Cordini is a member of the Baha'i faith. Her concept of God is an important part of her beliefs. "The more you explore the concept of God as a wholeness, the simpler it is to understand, and far more beautiful," she says. "It doesn't take away from religious beliefs. It accentuates them. When you embrace the wholeness, there's no hate, no negativity, no prejudice. You're in service of the All."

Cordini believes that her light-being self gathers information while her three-dimensional body is asleep, and she is committed to passing that knowledge to her fellow humans.

"Humans are just the little guys down here," she says. "They're just starting off in this vast exploration. It's going to be a rough road if they don't detach from the material point of view.

"When people think of the UFO phenomenon, they think of little green men and flying saucers," she adds. "I think of understanding, of cosmic awareness, of family, of teachers. I think of spiritual development as being open and free."

Cordini, who has done several nationwide radio interviews, says she is generally treated respectfully. No crank calls have come into the Intergalactic Contact Center phone line. Most callers just want to talk to someone. Others are confused by their own experiences. One or two have been what Cordini, who works in the mental health field, calls "delusional." She says she tries to keep an open mind when dealing with callers, aware of the skepticism that makes so many people reluctant to share their experiences.

"This is why we started the Intergalactic Contact Center, to be available to people who are having any sort of paranormal experience," she says. "I don't make any judgment about real or not real. To me, a person has experiences that are real to them. When people talk to me for the first time, I give them the option of seeking mental health help if that's what they need. I try to get people to search out their own experiences, but support is our main goal."

The journey may indeed be endless, but no one has to travel it alone.

Is This a Piece of an Extraterrestrial Craft?
by Jason Offutt

September-October 2008

Bob White found something strange in 1985. He can explain it, and often does, but people don't take him seriously. That is something he can't explain. The object he found is metallic, about seven and a half inches long, and resembles petrified wood. What makes it special to White is that he saw it ejected from a strange light … a light he's certain was a UFO.

"This thing came down out of the sky," said White, 77, of Reeds Spring, Missouri. "It was glowing like it was on fire. There's no doubt in my mind it wasn't anything of this earth. It couldn't be."

White took the object to government lab after government lab, including Los Alamos National Laboratory, and after two decades of being brushed off, someone is taking him seriously.

Mark W. Allin of The Above Network (an Internet discussion board on alternative news topics that boasts 127,794 members, www.AboveTopSecret.com) has come to White's aid, partly because he knows an object like this has been seen before.

It Gets Bizarre

"When you take into account the eyewitness testimony of Bob, who has passed three polygraph tests, this object becomes very unique," Allin said. "When you add the discovery of a formerly classified military report that describes an extremely similar event that also produced an object that is extremely similar to the Bob White object, it just gets bizarre."

White is convinced that the object was made by an intelligence not of this earth. "Everything points in the direction of extraterrestrials. Most of the analysis says that this thing is nothing organic from anything in or outside of earth's atmosphere. There's no explanation whatsoever."

Until Allin stepped in, that's where White's evidence ended. Although a few scientists have agreed to look at the object, White can't find one who'll say what it is, at least, not on the record.

"It's been analyzed by eight major labs, including Los Alamos (in 1996). I was told by one of the older scientists it was extraterrestrial, definitely. Then he later denied he said it. His bosses told him not to even talk about it."

That's one of the points that intrigued Allin: the mystery. Why have all the labs, all the scientists, given different answers?

"I remembered reading about this thing years ago and wanted to see if anything conclusive had been determined about it. Turns out that Larry Cekander, Bob's close friend, joined the discussion (on www.AboveTopSecret.com) and told us about all the conflicting reports and test results they had received," Allin said. "After reading about all of that I decided it might be a good idea to apply the resources of The Above Network toward getting a definitive answer as to what this thing is, where it came from, and how old it is."

According to a report from Colm Kelleher of the National Institute for Discovery Science, tests conducted at New Mexico Tech in 1996 showed the object was close in composition to a commercial aluminum casting alloy. "There are no anomalies in the results of this analysis," the report stated.

Friedman Convinced

The test results were good enough for nuclear physicist Stanton Friedman, author of the UFO books *Crash at Corona* and *Top Secret/Majic*. "I was very favorably impressed with the testing procedures and results and can't argue with their conclusion that it was a more or less standard aluminum alloy with silicon and other materials," Friedman said. "The composition, hardness, density, etc., all seemed to check out. I have no reason to doubt Bob's story, but see no reason to say that the material is clearly of ET origin."

But White has always contested the New Mexico Tech tests, and The Above Network has enlisted an independent Ph.D. metallurgist who has agreed to analyze White's object. Allin said he's not interested in bringing more attention to the object; he just wants to find out what it is and where it's from. "There is a lot of speculation that the results of some of the previous tests were not presented accurately. By hiring an independent scientist who answers to no one but himself we will be certain the results of his work will be genuine and accurate."

But after reviewing the results of previous tests, Allin's independent Ph.D. metallurgist decided in January that more analysis wasn't necessary.

"The recommendation is not to pursue any additional testing since the object possesses low-quality metallurgic properties, exhibits low-quality processing, and test results show that it originated from the earth," Allin wrote in an e-mail.

White is not satisfied with the metallurgist's recommendation. "ATS did not do any tests as they said they were going to. All they did was a review of others."

Hard Evidence?

White has asked his debunkers, if this is a manufactured object of earth origin, to make one themselves. So far, he has no takers. "As of yet, no reply from anyone," he said. "So since I am the only man who can make one, I guess this makes me the smartest man in the world, huh?"

Former president of the Institute for UFO Research, Franklin Carter, now a member of the Disclosure Project and the Mutual UFO Network, is familiar with White and is puzzled by the problems he's faced. "I know he's had a difficult time in trying to get someone to help him in the UFO community. You'd think with all the clamor for hard evidence, people would be crawling all over themselves to get to it."

Carter was involved with a UFO contactee conference hosted by the University of Wyoming when he met White.

"I believe his story," Carter said. "I have no question he found this thing and it fell off something in the sky."

Carter, who works in the animal pharmaceutical industry, also tried to get a scientist to look at White's object.

"I had some excellent contacts," he said. "I talked to some of them about it. 'Well, we don't want to get involved in UFOs, but we'll get you the data' ... I'm still waiting."

White said the object heats and cools rapidly and picks up radio signals, both AM and FM. And, during a UFO convention in Nevada, it disabled the electronics in a casino's hotel safe—three times.

"They ordered us not to walk through the casino with it," White said.

White briefly opened the Museum of the Unexplained in Reeds Spring, with his object as the centerpiece, but didn't make enough money to keep the museum open.

Things changed for White in 2000 when he received information about a government report from the 1940s made available in 1998 through the Freedom of Information Act. The report, "Flying Saucer from Denmark," describes an object almost identical to White's in appearance and composition that was recovered in the 1940s.

"This Thing Was Ejected… "

It wasn't just the laboratory denial that got Allin and Carter interested in White's case; it was his whole story.

While driving through Colorado at 2:00 a.m., White and a friend saw a light on the roadside near the Utah border. The light, White said, shouldn't have been there.

"It was a huge light on the ground," White said. "The light I saw was the size of a three-story building."

From the passenger seat, White watched his friend slow the car. "She was scared."

White's friend turned off the engine and headlights. "We coasted as close to this item as we could. She didn't want to stop, but we did."

They sat in the car, looking at the light. After a while, White's friend turned the headlights back on.

"Then the thing shot up in the sky," White said. The light went on to merge with other lights hovering in the sky. "It was two tubular neon lights with a blue light in between. The other light shot across the sky and disappeared in seconds. I know we don't have anything that moves that fast or that silently."

As the lights streaked across the sky, another light, small and orange, broke free and fell to earth.

"This thing was ejected from it," White said. "If this thing had just fallen it would have shot miles from me. It came down at an angle and kind of skimmed the hillside. When I came across it, it was still glowing."

Bob White's book *UFO Hard Evidence* and DVD *The Bob White Experience* are available at his website, www .hardevidence.info, along with a petition for a "Congressional Hearing on the Bob White Evidence."

Accepting My ET Heritage
by Rita Milios

January-February 2011

As a psychotherapist, I know that our subconscious minds can hide things from us until we are ready to safely integrate the hidden knowledge into our worldview. Never was this capacity more evident to me than the day I discovered that I had ET ancestors.

I've always thought of myself as an average person, more or less. Oh, I knew there was something a little different about me, but I figured that my difficult childhood contributed to my intense nature and seriousness. As a child I felt like a very old person. I seemed to be able to understand things beyond my years. I could understand other people's problems, even though they might be quite different from my own. Although I don't recall a lot about my childhood (apparently having suppressed much of it), I do recall an overall feeling of being very old inside, as if I were just waiting for time to pass and my body to grow so that I could begin to "do my job" (whatever that was to be).

I recall at age 13 feeling very lonely and helpless, wondering if I should just give up, or if I had it in me to hang on for another five years until I could leave my unhappy childhood behind and take charge of my own life. During one of my many solitary walks, I heard a voice that seemed to come from somewhere in the air surrounding me. It said, loudly and clearly, "You must hang on. You must survive. You have a job to do, and it has to do with how the universe works."

Wow! That was a big assignment—and certainly worth waiting for. So I steeled myself for the long, hard years to come and waited to grow up.

Intuitive Messages

After that, my life was directed by occasional intuitive messages that were so strong that I knew they must be heeded. Almost always, they came with unexpected surprises as well. Once, when I was presenting a workshop in Dayton, Ohio, I met another speaker with whom I immediately identified. We both felt an immediate rapport, as if our energies had somehow connected. During my speech, I felt an outpouring of universal energy come into my body and then flow out into the audience. I realized that this other person's energy had been a catalyst; it had opened my solar plexus chakra completely, allowing the universal energy to flow through me unimpeded and connect me with my audience at a deeply emotional level.

This person was on my Path for another reason as well. Through her I learned about hypnotherapy and realized immediately that this was something that I should do. Three days later, I was enrolled in my first hypnotherapy class. I then went on to take several advanced classes, one of which led to my first, and most profound, ET experience.

During this particular hypnotherapy course, we were learning the technique of doing past-life regressions. I had always avoided getting a past life regression myself, even though I had been teaching spiritual classes for about eight years at the time. My reasoning was that I didn't have any unexplained problems that would lead me to believe that a traumatic past life needed to be cleared up. Besides, I hadn't found anyone whom I felt I could trust to do it (even though I knew of a psychologist who did past life regressions). Nonetheless, at this point, want it or not, I was getting a regression, as we students always practiced on one another.

UFO Nightmare

Six weeks before the day of the regression, I began to experience intense anxiety whenever I thought about the upcoming event. I was inexplicably tense, literally shaking in my boots. Not only that, I began to have a feeling of dread and the return of a recurring childhood nightmare where lights filled the sky and I knew that these were the lights of UFOs. I knew, too, that they had come to get me, along with many other people who were also huddled behind the large rocks in a field. (Yes, this sounds very much like *Close Encounters of the Third Kind*, but trust me, these dreams occurred several decades prior to the movie coming out.) In my dream, my biggest fear as I awaited the UFO landing was that I would soon be leaving my family behind and would be all alone, among strange "people" in a strange place.

Shortly before the weekend of the past-life regression, we did another hypnotherapy session where the technique was to deal with the biggest fear in your life. At the time, I wasn't thinking about the UFO dream but was shocked and terrified to go into a hypnotic vision where I saw a spaceship, with a little man emerging and walking toward me. I was so fearful that my hypnosis-training partner had to incorporate several safety techniques to allow me to feel comfortable enough to talk to him. (We put him behind Plexiglass and kept him at a distance.) He told me that I had a job to do (this had become a familiar phrase to me) and that even though I was afraid, I should not worry because I had previously agreed to do this job, in full knowledge of what it entailed. I had made a commitment and a sacrifice, which I was just now fully realizing. The little spaceman said these things to me; then he left.

The Promise

Immediately, within my body, there was a deep relaxation, a sigh of relief. If I had made a promise, fine. I would keep it. I knew instinctively that this would have some later connection to the past-life regression, but now I was resigned to it. I had an extreme sense of commitment about keeping promises; it was a lifelong value that I had held ever since

I could remember. I knew it was not something that I had ever decided to do; it had simply always been a fundamental part of my being. I also knew that this commitment would lead me to a positive place, no matter how scary it might be to get there.

Too soon, the weekend of the past-life regression came, and with it, the return of my fears. Yes, I would go through with the regression, but not happily. That Friday evening as I arrived in Dayton I was a nervous wreck. The next morning we were going to do the regression. That night as I was lying in my bed in a hotel room, studying for an upcoming hypnosis exam, I was suddenly overcome by the feeling of a presence trying to reach me. I knew that in a moment's time I could be channeling this presence and finding out what it wanted, but I felt very anxious about making the contact. Intuition told me that it had to do with the regression and I wanted to wait and deal with that when I had my fellow students as protection. The presence was, however, so intense and so distracting that I finally thought, Okay, let me just allow a little of it to come in, so that I can drain off some of this excess energy and then get back to work. No sooner had the thought ended, when I was overcome by a vision of being in a deep forest. Only I wasn't just seeing the vision, I was in it.

I was looking up into the sky. Just ahead at treetop level was a large white light. It was a UFO but it was going, not coming. I was overwhelmed with grief. I was sobbing, crying buckets of tears, reaching out in pitiful desperation. "They're leaving me! They're leaving me behind! My people! My people! They're leaving me behind!" I cried over and over, sobbing into my pillow so as not to wake anyone who might be in the next room.

Gumby

About this time, as some fragment of my conscious mind was grasping the meaning of these words, I began to envision and to feel the physical presence of an ET. He was similar to the "Gumby" types depicted in some books—long, thin body, tendril-like fingers, and an egg-shaped head. He had wonderful, loving, large dark eyes. He was just in front of me and to my left. He was telling me, "I'm sorry. I'm so sorry. I never wanted to leave you. We tried to wait for you but we couldn't any longer." (He was apologizing for leaving me behind. Evidently, if an ET lingered too long in Earth's dense vibrations, their own vibrations would decrease and they could become "held" by Earth's magnetic field.) "You knew this was a possibility," he continued, "when you accepted the task." (I somehow intuited that this was to "seed" the earth—and I got the impression that this had taken place millions of years ago at the dawn of life on earth.) "You agreed to take the risk," he reminded me. "But I always loved you. I didn't leave you on purpose. I've missed you so much."

Then he began to touch my face, my arms, my hands, and to caress me as a loved one would. He told me that he was my father (or rather, had been at that earlier time period) and that it was he who had visited me in the previous hypnotic session. He said that the time had come for me to realize who and what I was, to reclaim my heritage.

I'm Not an ET!

Forget it! That's what I thought. No way did I want to be an ET. I'd worked very hard in my life to maintain an image of normalcy as I went about my metaphysical work, while also keeping up a professional, clinical persona. I valued my traditional image, as it lent credibility to my "alternative" research and writing endeavors. I didn't want to spoil my image by accepting such a way-out idea.

But the trance had been so immediate, so strong, and so undeniable, that I had no choice but to entertain the possibility that it might be true. The next day, during my past-life regression hypnosis session, I revisited the scene and went through a somewhat less traumatic version of the same event. "Frederick" (not his real name he said, but what my Gumby-like ET friend told me to call him) said that if I would allow it, he could become a part of my aura. He would be with me from that moment on to guide me and to help me.

I agreed (sort of) and then he began to hang around in my aura, at about the level of my right shoulder. At first I was very wary, but it felt comforting to have him there and I soon came to enjoy it. About a year later, I came to fully accept his ET presence. Frederick now resides in me and is truly a part of me. I feel him in my heart.

Kundalini Rising

This final merging took place in a semi-dream state as I was falling off to sleep one night. I began to experience a movement of energy within my chakras, starting at the base of my spine. (I later recognized this as a kundalini rising event.) I felt a vibration within each chakra in turn, starting with the first chakra and proceeding through the seventh, with a continuing rising up of the energies from each chakra below as the process continued.

I had previously participated in chakra exercises and had felt the movement of kundalini energy before, but this was happening without my even having to focus my attention on the areas. The effect was so strong that I became fully awake. As the energy flowed upward it would stop for a few moments at each chakra. I felt throughout this process a sense of integration, of finally having full energy flow available between all my chakras. I knew instinctively that this experience would lead to positive results, but what these would be, I had no clue.

When my crown chakra energy finally had been integrated with the rest, I felt Frederick move from my aura into my body, first overlaying me and then settling down into my heart. I felt totally at peace with this move and accepted him fully. At that moment I realized that I had accepted and integrated a previously separated part of my soul. By discovering who I was, I had become more of who I am.

Valued Heritage

Now, many years later, I value my ET heritage, rather than fear it. I have been privileged to meet and help clients who also have an ET heritage. I know that this ancestry has contributed greatly to my abilities as an intuitive, a counselor, a healer, and a human being. And for that I will always be grateful to my ET elders.

FOUR: Speculation

Since at least the early 1950s, conventional wisdom has decided that UFOs are either (1) delusions and fakes or (2) space vehicles from another world. But this is a false dichotomy; there could be any number of other explanations. Speculation is rife. Unfortunately, there is a tendency is some quarters to suppress any data or reports that do not support the extraterrestrial hypothesis (or ETH). Personally, this strikes me as rather close-minded and non-productive. Since it has been more than sixty years since the Arnold sighting and we still have no proven explanations, perhaps it is time to consider more than one possibility.

There has been some discussion of the "Watchers." These are mentioned in the Bible, where they are called Nephilim, translated in the King James Bible as "giants." Scott Corrales elucidates how this tale has become somewhat extrapolated into a story about extraterrestrial aliens observing humanity and interbreeding with human females to produce hybrids with unusual abilities. The story has persisted on its own without reference to the Bible. I am personally acquainted with a man who claims to be such a hybrid himself. Aside from this, many people have seen very striking similarities between reports of encounters with ETs or MIB and those with elves, fairies, angels, or demons. Could all these be the same phenomenon seen from different perspectives? Virginia Tilly points out that UFO sightings and close encounters are very frequently associated with paranormal phenomena of all kinds and wonders if UFOs themselves might fall into the same category as clairvoyance and psychokinesis. Nigel Watson notes the close resemblance between meeting aliens and the reported encounters of medieval witches with Satan or his representatives, not to mention the even more shocking resemblance between the experiences of abductees and the initiatory journeys of shamans.

Another explanation of UFOs, even farther from the ETH, is that they are themselves unknown creatures living in our atmosphere. Brad Steiger here explores that idea and recounts an encounter with a UFO that behaved much more like an individual entity than a nuts-and-bolts spacecraft.

Finally, authors and investigators James Moseley and the late Karl T. Pflock, authors of the highly informative Shockingly Close to the Truth, debate whether UFOs are alien hardware or extradimensional phenomena of an almost supernatural nature.supernatural nature.

Are UFOs Alive?
By Brad Steiger

September-October 2010

Fay Clark, the publisher of Hiawatha Books, who died on October 23, 1991, was an early mentor of mine. When I was just beginning to seriously explore the strange, the unusual, and the unknown, it seemed that Fay knew everyone in the psychic, paranormal, and UFO field from coast to coast. He opened many doors for me—and he opened corners of my mind that might have remained shut far longer if not for his guidance and inspiration.

An extra bonus for me was that Fay was an absolute dead-ringer for the great motion picture actor Claude Rains, even to his manner of speaking. Sometimes I truly felt as though I was receiving instruction from the Invisible Man, Sir John Talbot, or Mr. Jordan.

I want to share this remarkable account of a UFO sighting, circa 1973, from Fay in his own words:

"I had been investigating UFOs for 22 years, but the sighting that completely changed my view of the phenomenon occurred at Lone Pine, California. My wife and I observed a UFO resting on a small grove of aspen trees. We had been attracted to the area by a terrifically bright light that was so intense we were unable to look directly at it.

Clark's Account

"Then the light subsided somewhat and we could see the clear outline of the object. All the way around it were openings in its side. The light began to grow until it covered nearly the entire area of the object. As it grew in size, it lost its brilliance and became a lavender color. When the light reached nearly the entire size of the object, the illumination began to shrink down again until it got to the very brilliant white portion again, which, if my judgment were correct, would probably have been about 20 feet in diameter. Then the light would again increase its size to maybe three-quarters or four-fifths of the size of the entire object, and it would be that lavender color.

"This process of expansion and contraction of light continued, and my wife and I realized that it was matching the rhythm of our respiration rate.

"We became aware that the object was increasing its tempo. We saw one edge of the UFO raise so that it was no longer level with the tops of the trees. In the length of time that it took me to turn my head, the object had moved 10 miles out over Death Valley. I know it was 10 miles, because we drove out underneath it.

"The thing that really amazed my wife and me was that it took off at that tremendous speed instantly—with no sound, no fire, no smoke. And all of the trees leaned with it. They were not blasted backward. We looked the area over carefully and found no more small limbs and leaves on the ground than one would find under any grove of trees.

"The word that kept coming to me was that the object was impelled, rather than propelled. It was drawn, rather than pushed. If there would have been any force pushing it, it certainly would have blasted limbs and leaves off the trees.

"We drove out in the desert and stayed with the object for probably an hour and a half, directly underneath it. When we first stopped the car, some substance that looked like whipped cream or heavy fog rolled out of the openings in its sides. It was probably not over 300 feet above the ground, but it was completely hidden from view after it produced its own "cloud" of this substance.

"We knew it was there, though, so we drove back a distance so that we could clearly see it sitting on top of its artificial cloud.

It's Alive!

"What we were observing, I believe, was a phenomenon going on inside the object. I believe that the thing was breathing, and I see no reason to change my thought on that matter.

"My wife and I both had the feeling that we were witnessing the ultimate in creation. The closer we came to the object, the more we were suffused with a feeling of reverence and beauty and humbleness.

"I'll tell about another object we witnessed, and I will illustrate why I know there were no occupants inside it. This sighting occurred outside of Seligman, Arizona. We watched the object coming, then observed it change its course to come to hover not more than 15 feet above our Volkswagen. It seemed to me that it was just looking at us, as if it were studying our little car.

"I jumped out with my Hasselblad camera and swung it up to take a picture. But before I could even touch the shutter, the UFO zipped right toward a little butte.

"I had a terrible, sick feeling that anything so beautiful was going to crash and be destroyed. Instead of crashing, though, just before it touched the butte it shot straight up. It didn't stop; it just changed direction—a right angle, straight up—and disappeared.

"No crew could have been in any craft and survived such a maneuver. They would have been mashed against the sides of the vehicle, then pulled apart by the acceleration straight up.

"I do not believe that we observed a craft made by beings from some other planet. I believe that we were watching a living creature, a form of life that moves into our dimension.

"Different people throughout the years have said to me, 'Fay, you know a lot more than you are telling. Come on now, tell us the truth. Admit that you made contact with the aliens inside the object. At least tell us they contacted you.'

"But, Brad, we were not contacted; and there were no occupants inside the object. We only had the most wonderful feeling of peace and harmony, and the knowledge that we were witnessing the beauty of the ultimate of creation.

"I firmly believe that UFOs are a form of life that come not from another planet but from another dimension. I believe that they are probably all around us all the time—just outside of our own dimension.

Extradimensional Forms

"When I discussed the matter of living UFOs with another old friend, Trevor James Constable, he said that biological life in the upper octave of terrestrial existence has been overlooked by too many UFO investigators who early on were in favor of the foregone conclusion that UFOs were vehicles from outer space.

"T. J. handed me a stack of photos of UFOs that he had taken with a Leica G IR 135 infrared film at f–3.5, 1/30.

"'These are plainly biological forms,' he said. 'These are plasmic living organisms native to our atmosphere. As they appear in these photographs, they give one the impression of looking through the side of an aquarium.'

Barometric Pressure Wave

"Constable continued: 'The daily etheric breathings of the Earth produce a barometric pressure wave twice daily, which formal science has never been able to explain. There is enough energy in these barometric waves to run the world's machines—if we can but find the transducer. The torque drive of the Earth itself is an inexhaustible, life-positive energy source of staggering magnitude. That's what civilization depends on—making material substance spin. We see the discs in our skies manifesting these spinning motions over and over again, pressed down upon us in such profusion that one wonders how there can be any vestige of skepticism remaining. Wilhelm Reich has already shown that motors can be run directly from the cosmic life energy, also called orgone, as he discovered and refined that energy.

"'The characteristic of this coming epoch—heralded by UFOs—is that free primary energy will run the world. No one can put etheric force into a wire and sell it. No sheik can say that tomorrow etheric force is going to cost four times what it does today. No one can confine it within storage tanks and demand money for it. Everyone is going to have energy to do the world's work without pollution and without financial price.

"'Before long, someone will uncover that all-important step (discovered by Wilhelm Reich but not disclosed by him) by which etheric force can be transduced into existing electric motors or simple adaptations of them. Orgone and magnetism are cheek by jowl. The UFO evidence screams this at the world. The era of free primary energy is imminent, and its imminence is reinforced by the absolute necessity for its appearance. The UFO shows the feasibility and potential of etheric force in technological use. With etheric force comes not just a new technical epoch, but a cultural and educational change forced by the need to understand etheric energies as we now understand other energy forms.

"'The price for this new technical epoch is a forced overhaul of our whole mode of existence. We will see the beginning of a reunion between science and religion as the cosmic energies—pervaded with life and themselves the milieu of living beings—come into technical utility. Man will find the central parts of his own physical existence inseparably bound up with etheric energies, and he will be opened to a widened understanding of himself and the cosmos that produced him. The ultimate consequence will be a new humanity.'"

Do UFOs Have a Metaphysical Aspect?
By Virginia M. Tilly

May-June 2009

Untold amounts of high-strangeness UFO-abduction information has been ignored, rejected, or never even noted. When an investigator is told by a UFO witness, "I had the feeling that I was being watched," it has been dismissed as the thinking of an attention-seeking individual. In gathering data there is typically no place to record much in the way of subjective reality.

The percipient may relate to the investigator: "This may sound crazy, but just before this happened I had a sudden urge to go for a walk," despite the fact that it was after dark on a clear, quiet weeknight. The excursion inexplicably leads to some deserted place, such as a field or an empty parking lot.

The supposedly least credible witness of all is the one who reports repeated UFO sightings. It seems illogical that while most people never see a UFO (even if they want to or try to) others see several of them.

Openings such as these, however, provide an observant investigator with an opportunity to ask questions of a more metaphysical nature. Most researchers are committed to gathering information about physical reality only: Can it be measured? Weighed? Disassembled? Analyzed? Photographed? They remain faithful to the modern Western world's dedication to reductionistic science.

Speaking to his colleagues at Harvard University in 1895, psychologist and philosopher William James said, "There is included in human nature an ingrained naturalism and materialism of mind which can only admit facts that are actually tangible. Of this sort of mind the entity called 'Science' is the idol. Fondness for the word scientist is one of the notes by which you may recognize its votaries; and its short way of killing any position it disbelieves is to call it unscientific."

We live in an era in which the scientific view has been that the supernatural, or paranormal, cannot exist; therefore, it does not exist. Thus, either no attempt, or only a very cursory one is made at explaining unusual phenomena. More frequently that type of information has just been ignored. In far too many instances the subjective facts have not even been collected.

Pressures for the Investigators

There are so many elements of the UFO phenomenon that are illogical, unreasonable, unbelievable, or just too weird to be given serious consideration by scientific observers. It is not surprising that the door has been closed to investigating or even contemplating the most paranormal claims of UFO and abduction percipients. An investigator who wants to be taken seriously rarely includes details that seem more appropriate for ghost hunters, parapsychologists, New Agers, or even demonologists and exorcists.

Only a few intrepid investigators have gathered information in UFO reports about the metaphysical aspects of this phenomenon, such as psychokinesis, materializations and dematerializations, levitation, mental telepathy, clairaudience, clairvoyance, clairsentience, synchronicities, religious visions, or even anomalous animals.

An Unparalleled Enigma

Jacques Vallée is a scientist well known for his investigations into the absurdities (or "metalogic") of the UFO phenomenon. In his evaluation of the metaphysical aspects involved, he has said: "The key to an understanding of the UFO phenomenon may lie in the psychic effects it produces (or the awareness it makes possible) in some observers; whose lives are deeply changed and who develop unusual talents with which they may find it difficult to cope..."

Individuals who have close encounters and/or abduction experiences are sometimes frightened, sometimes confused, but always amazed by phenomena that happen to and around them, or by what they themselves are suddenly able to do. Curiously, many investigators begin to experience anomalies in their own lives as they become more involved in these high strangeness cases.

UFO craft exhibit puzzling aspects, such as their seeming ability to defy the laws of physics as we currently understand them. They travel at incredible speeds, hover silently, morph into different shapes, and seem to defy gravity. In the blink of an eye, they appear and disappear. Even with our best stealth technology we cannot render objects invisible.

In CE IIIs and CE IVs (close encounters of the third and fourth kinds), there is a great probability that the sudden disappearance of a craft at close range is the point at which an apparent abductee is "switched off," then "on" by the force with which they have been interacting.

ET Seems to Be Able to Materialize and Dematerialize
The entities associated with UFOs also display incredible abilities. Often these seem to be passed on to the human in such cases.

These beings seem to materialize and dematerialize before the witnesses' eyes. On several occasions I have had abductees attempt to describe what that looks like. Some have explained it as dissolving either in midair or in a misty haze. Others say they twinkle or sparkle as they seem to disintegrate.

After hearing many such descriptions, I was amazed when I read in an older book the following account: "I heard a peculiar rumbling sound ... His body began to melt gradually within the piercing light. First his feet and legs vanished, then his torso and head ... faded; nothing remained before me but the ... window and a pale stream of sunlight."

On another occasion the same author wrote: "There was a sudden flash; we witnessed the instantaneous dechemicalization of the electronic elements of [his] body into a spreading vaporous light ... trillions of tiny ... sparks faded into the infinite reservoir."

That passage from *Autobiography of a Yogi* by Paramahansa Yogananda relates the disappearance of the spiritual entity with whom Yogananda had interacted on numerous occasions early in the 20th century.

Isn't That Impossible?

Another metaphysical aspect displayed by these beings is the ability to pass through walls, roofs, and closed doors or windows, often with a human in tow.

Almost every abductee has at least one of these episodes to relate. Several have told how they tried to stiffen their bodies and pull back as they were being escorted toward a solid wall. The next thing they knew, they were on the other side without having felt anything.

One unusual case involved a woman who told me that while lying in her bed one night she felt herself being drawn through a bedroom window head first, face down, arms pulled back at her sides. She could feel the glass as it seemed to drag across her face and body until she was out to about her waist. It seemed to her that something was not quite right. She had gone through walls and windows before without feeling anything.

The next thing she knew, her direction reversed, and in a moment she was back in her room. She found herself almost immediately moving out the window again, this time quickly and without the earlier sense of drag across her face and body.

One very young girl asked her abductors how they could take her so easily through a closed door. Her guide told her that it was actually quite simple, but human scientific knowledge was rather primitive, so we did not yet understand how this was accomplished. He added that very soon humans would begin to understand how to do this and much more.

Anomalous Animals Connected with Abductions

Another perplexing phenomenon associated with UFOs and abductions is the presence of anomalous animals. Out-of-place or oversized animals, Sasquatch-type beings, mixed-species entities, or even mythological animals may be observed in the general area of UFO sightings or around people who have sightings or abductions. This can occur before, during, and after UFO activity.

Most frequently reported is a black panther, always totally outside of its natural habitat. Occasionally a green lizard-man or a Mothman-type entity is observed. Localized reports of similar encounters are typically given by several independent witnesses.

I have collected several reports of Sasquatch-type creatures. One of my most interesting came from a 14-year-old boy. A few days after I had been on a local radio program talking about UFOs, one of my students approached me after school and cautiously asked if he could tell me about something that had happened to him. On a cold January night the previous year, he had suddenly decided to go for a walk. He noticed a very bright light in the sky that seemed to follow him. Before long he heard a soft beeping sound. He remembered little else from that night, and remained quite puzzled by it.

After telling me about this event he asked if I believed in Bigfoot. When I assured him that I felt that there had to be something to all of the sightings, he told me that on several occasions he had seen such a creature. Curiously, it always seemed to be observing him. This happened when he was visiting his grandmother in a remote area of Michigan's Upper Peninsula.

Unusual Animals in the "Zone of Strangeness"

As an individual is drawn into the zone of strangeness, he may encounter a hauntingly attractive or compelling animal. Two most frequently reported are a deer or an extremely large owl. The animal is suddenly observed directly in view, usually remaining motionless while staring intently at the human with large, dark, mesmerizing eyes. Typically this is one of the last things remembered before a missing-time experience occurs.

I suspect that these and other animals (ravens, wolves, butterflies, or bees) may be a form of screen memory used to distract a human at the beginning of an abduction experience. In some cases, they may even be shapeshifters.

Why are so many of these unusual animals observed by UFO witnesses and abductees? Is the creature some part of the UFO phenomenon? Is this some form of energy or force attracted for some reason to people who have these experiences? Is it possible that the experiencer is viewing another dimension or reality? Or is it even possible that the individual herself is creating or releasing an energy by which they materialize?

Men in Black Make Appearances Too

Another long-standing curiosity connected with these experiences is the phenomenon of MIBs, or Men in Black. These unusual beings were common in the 1950s and '60s, and rarely heard of in the '70s and '80s. They are again more frequently reported.

People who encounter MIBs are those who have had close encounters of the first, second, and third kinds, abductees (the fourth kind), as well as UFO investigators. In most cases the targeted person is alone when she is visited by one, or more typically three, of them. Almost always male, they are described as being either pale-skinned, almost colorless, or as having an Oriental complexion and facial characteristics.

Usually only one individual speaks. The voice is often a flat, expressionless monotone. Many say that somehow they do not seem real with their stiff, awkward movements. Frequently they do not seem to understand how to operate fairly simple devices. They are dressed in a black suit, white shirt, black tie, a brimmed black hat, and dark sunglasses.

If a vehicle is observed it is typically a late model, immaculate, large black car, generally a Cadillac. When license numbers have been recorded and checked out, there is never such a registration in existence. Invariably a message is delivered to the human about knowing too much, getting out of this field of research, or not talking about it with anyone.

Black Helicopters as MIBs?

In recent years, UFO investigators and abductees have had repeated close encounters with large, black, unmarked helicopters. These are generally Hueys equipped with a special antenna. There are no identifying numbers, marks, or insignia anywhere on these craft. Even the windows are so dark that when seen at close range it is impossible to observe who (or what) is inside. They fly illegally, making low passes, circling or hovering over populated areas, all without proper identification.

The Rev. Barry Downing has suggested that these may not really be helicopters. Many people are beginning to consider these helicopters to be the modern version of the Men in Black. They feel that those who control the supposed helicopters are trying to intimidate and scare them away from learning anything more about UFOs.

While I have personally had several experiences with black helicopters, I have never felt intimidated or threatened by them. I do, however, resent their intrusion into my personal life and I feel very closely observed.

A curious sidelight to this issue can be found in an entry in *Harper's Encyclopedia*, stating that in "Eastern mysticism the MIBs have a parallel in the 'Brothers of the Shadow,' evil beings who try to prevent occult students from learning the great truth."

Mind Control

An abundance of evidence about close encounters shows that there is intense control of the human mind during an abduction experience. Whatever the method used to achieve this control, an experiencer is inexplicably and suddenly influenced to act or to think in certain ways. While driving he may suddenly, without provocation, turn down a deserted road. Or he may, during a solo walk, unexpectedly go into a wooded area or to a lonely park.

Or he may awaken to become aware that there is an intruder going into a sleeping child's room. He first thinks: *I must get up and go to my child's room to protect her!*, but then inexplicably concludes: *Oh, everything's okay. I'll just go back to sleep now.* Invariably in the morning the child relates a very strange dream or memories of some strange being at his or her bedside during the night.

Abductees report that as much as 100 percent of the communication during their experiences is done telepathically. Most abductees report having heard their names called telepathically at the beginning of the encounter. Only rarely is the name heard aurally. Their name may be repeated over and over until they respond in some manner. On some occasions as an individual is recalling having heard that voice (usually reported as sounding male and only occasionally as having a mechanical sound quality), they become agitated and say something like, "He's inside my head!"

Frequently abductees explain how, in their terror, they mentally struggle with, challenge, or question their captors. Many recall having been given the thought that their resistance makes the experience much more complicated and unpleasant than it needs to be. Many of them are led to believe that their mental resistance also led to controlling and ending the experience. This may be another example of a screen memory—a false memory that masks a traumatic one.

Most percipients report that post-abduction changes include being able to use telepathy in their daily lives. Many report being able to think of someone and have them call or appear in a short time. Or they send mundane messages (e.g., "Bring me a candy bar") to someone who then, without knowing or even wondering why, responds in the appropriate manner. Some claim that they can look into the eyes of another person and read what is in his thoughts.

Development of Clairaudience

Closely associated with telepathy is clairaudience, the clear or acute perception of sounds, music, and voices from no apparent external source. Many abductees begin to experience such skills at an early age. While most do not associate it with their close encounters, there are too many commonalities among these incidents to ignore the connection.

Clairaudience includes being given messages while in a dreamlike state, just before falling asleep or waking. Most clairaudience is perceived as an internal voice distinctly different from one's own.

Many abductees report hearing music in their heads, something quite different from having a catchy song or jingle on your mind. It seems to be received internally as though it were a recording playing. It usually comes as a surprise, then suddenly shuts off.

Abductees frequently hear their names called, again internally. This has been going on for centuries. King Solomon heard his name called, as did Moses and Samuel, and also Mohammed, Socrates, and Joan of Arc. The contacted individual is usually told to go to a certain location or to engage in a particular activity, like cleaning up the Earth's environment or to improving one's eating habits. Others report being forewarned about disasters or other approaching events.

We can only wonder what may be involved with those who hear voices that tell them to preach or to start cults. Some have been instructed to arm themselves heavily and to gain complete mental and physical control of their followers and as many other souls as possible. It is clear that not all such communication is of a positive or constructive nature. Furthermore, not all messages are meaningful—and some are downright dishonest.

Do Abductees Also Become Clairvoyant?

Clairvoyance is defined in *Harper's Encyclopedia of Mystical and Paranormal Experiences* as "The perception of current objects, events, or people that may not be discerned through the normal senses." It "may manifest in internal or external visions, or a sensing of images."

Many percipients relate experiences that they or their family members have had which could be called clairvoyance.

On several occasions, one woman would envision a car, complete with license number, and within hours see that exact car. The same woman had a vision of a house on a vacant field across the road. She said it sat at an odd angle and had rather unique windows. Within a year, the land had been sold and the house, exactly as she had seen it, was constructed.

Another woman became frantic when, at our scheduled meeting time, I arrived at her home relating how I had just witnessed a small plane crashing. I calmed her, reassuring her that everything was okay. The only person in the plane, the pilot, had crawled out with only minor injuries. That was not the problem, she told me.

She had had a dream a few days earlier about my coming in and telling her exactly what I had just related.

Later that day, this woman's husband was scheduled to be released from a brief stay in a local hospital. The night before he had told her that after their now 22-month-old son had been born, he had known that after a second child was born he himself would be hospitalized. He added that it would not be serious and that he would be home in a short time.

More than a year before, his wife had had another of her clairvoyant dreams. In that vision, their small son stood next to the rocking chair in which she sat holding a baby in her arms. The older boy asked, "Mommy, when is Daddy coming home from the hospital?"

"Daddy is going to be fine," she assured him. "He'll be home in a few days."

This woman rarely discusses her dream-visions, as they usually involve emotionally charged events centered on people with whom she is very close.

Dealing with Clairsentience

Though rarely called by its more metaphysical name, clairsentience, many abductees report an acute psychic perception involving any or all of their physical senses: seeing, hearing, smelling, tasting, or touching, as well as emotions that become psychic and intuitive impressions.

Many abductees become aware up to several hours in advance that an abduction is going to take place. Often they hear a buzzing sound or tone in their heads. They have the disquieting feeling that someone is hovering nearby, watching and listening. Work and other activities are performed as if only going through the motions. They know that later that night they will once again be visited.

Children who have these feelings tend to become hyperactive, even aggressive, or withdrawn and moody. They may try to put off going to bed for as long as possible or try to sleep anywhere other than in their own bed. In abductee families, it is not uncommon to have a lot of bed-switching. Many will sleep on a sofa, the floor, a chair, or even on a table. Sometimes moving to another place to sleep seems to help, but usually it does not.

An individual may report a fleeting impression or feeling. Upon closer scrutiny this can be interpreted as a true instance of intuition, such as knowing which numbers to pick in the lottery or that there is a police car nearby when one is driving too fast.

A number of years ago, a percipient wanted to find another woman who had reported being assaulted and, as was not uncommon at the time, was being challenged by authorities. The percipient wanted to offer the victim moral and emotional support. With no idea how to find this woman, who lived in a remote rural area near a small village, she started driving, using gut-level instincts alone.

Without knowing why, at several places she suddenly turned onto various roads and within a remarkably short time found herself at the victim's home. After a brief explanation, she was warmly received.

Volumes could be filled with such experiences collected by open-minded investigators. Many have had such experiences themselves, whether or not they will admit to it publicly.

A serious-minded investigator was enthusiastically chasing a UFO across the countryside. When there was no longer a road to reach the area where the UFO hovered near the ground, he got out of his car. He climbed a fence and continued on foot across an open field, eager to experience his first close encounter.

Suddenly he stopped. He had a feeling that he should no longer continue. He hurried back to his car and left the scene without further thought. Afterwards he was dumfounded as to why he would have stopped this tantalizing pursuit.

Shouldn't Psychokinesis Be Impossible Too?

The ability of the mind to control the movement or activity of inanimate objects is known as *psychokinesis*. Not only do abductees report that their abductors display such powers, but many of them find that they too can use their own minds to do seemingly impossible things.

Doors and windows can be made to slam shut without anyone touching them. Lights may be dimmed, brightened, or turned off or on in the same inexplicable manner. Telephones, clocks, radios, televisions, and recording devices can have their operations disrupted or be turned off or on without a touch. Later they usually function normally once again.

Animals have been affected too. More than once I have heard an abductee describe how he has gotten an insect or some other creature to change directions by concentrating on it or pointing at it.

Psychokinesis is erratic for most people. It may be something like someone wondering what he should do next and at that instant a book falls off of a shelf displaying pertinent information. It appears that the stronger one's emotions are at the time, the more successful the psychokinetic effects become.

What Does It All Mean?

The lives of individuals having close encounters are filled with metaphysical phenomena. Others include miracles and healings, space-time distortions, synchronicities, shadowy entities, poltergeist-like activity, empathy, and out-of-body experiences.

Is it just coincidence that these experiences have a transformative effect upon those who are abducted? Do these metaphysical aspects connected with the UFO phenomenon have meaning, or is it just an accidental byproduct? Apparently, only time and additional research of these unusual experiences will reveal that answer.

Angels or Aliens? The Mysterious Biblical Struggles of Angels and Men
By Scott Corrales

December 2000

"I saw Watchers in my vision, a dream vision, and behold two of them argued about me … and they were engaged in a great quarrel concerning me. I asked them: 'You, why do you argue thus about me?' They answered and said to me: 'We have been made masters and rule over the sons of men.' And they said to me: 'Which of us do you choose? … '"

The preceding is a fragment from the "Testament of Amram," a document written in Aramaic that forms part of the Qumran scrolls, more commonly known as the Dead Sea Scrolls. The entire fragment, some eight patchy paragraphs, relates a story told by Moses' father, Amram, to his children, concerning the burden of choice: whether to serve the evil Watcher Melkiresha, a viper-faced demon, or his counterpart, the Watcher Melchizedek, who is ruler of the "Sons of Light."

Much has been made over the last few decades of the link between the role played by the biblical Watchers and that played by UFOs and their occupants, as well as the phenomena associated with them. This order of nonhuman beings, which fell from grace on account of their transgressions with "the daughters of men," are at the core of a current controversy. The viper-eyed Melkiresha, allegorical though it may be, is strangely reminiscent of some of the more reptilian UFO entities that have been reported in a number of encounters. The Watchers, as described in the Bible or by the Tibetan monks who discussed the topic with the Russian artist/mystic Nicholas Roerich (whose paintings of Asian hill-forts are often referred to in the writings of H. P. Lovecraft), are in essence a race of beings which have always lived in the skies and lord over humanity, reveling in intermarriage with humans. The biblical Noah, for example, was the offspring of a Watcher.

Mexican author Luis Ramírez Reyes describes interaction between the same kind of strange beings and humans taking place in our very own times. While the following report would perhaps be better filed under "alien aggression," there are certain elements that make it a more suitable fit for "interaction between humans and hostile spiritual agencies."

In 1993, Rafael Perrin, a television talk-show personality, was hosting a party one night at his apartment in Mexico City's swank Zona Rosa district. Around midnight, he stepped out onto his balcony to catch a breath of fresh air when, looking down to the sidewalk, he noticed a wounded dog lying on the sidewalk, twisting and howling. Moved by the sight, Perrin left his apartment to assist the suffering animal, but was prevented from touching the dog by a "young fellow dressed in rags," who in spite of his reduced circumstances did not act like a beggar. The youth told Perrin that a band of aliens roaming the streets of Mexico City had inflicted harm upon the canine with a small beam-emitting device they carried on them. Perrin was further astonished when the young beggar went into a lengthy discussion of the beam weapon's origin, its effect, the nature of the predatory aliens and the damage attributed to "unknown parties" that was common in the area. The youth was about to heal the suffering dog using a similar device which "reversed the effect" of the harmful beam.

Rather than staying to witness the miraculous cure, Perrin ran back up to his apartment to fetch his camcorder, hoping to capture on film the curing of an injured animal by means of nonhuman technology. But when he returned to the scene, the young beggar was nowhere in sight. Perrin saw only the no-longer-wounded dog walking away down the sidewalk. "Imagine how I regret not having remained to witness the way in which that person used the device and … listening to his accounts of how there were aliens among us, fighting and squabbling with each other over control of the earth."

Readers may take Perrin's story, as told to Ramírez Reyes, with a grain of salt, but note the similarity to biblical accounts of warring factions of angels (or the mysterious Watchers) and the propensity of angels to appear as young human males endowed with special powers.

In November 1991, Monica María Ortega, a young Colombian woman, told of a nocturnal sexual encounter with an alleged "alien" (which could well have been one of the Watchers) on a nationally syndicated TV show. Far from being one of the current crop of Greys, her nonhuman lover was more in step with the traditional sky people, elementals, or other creatures who have interacted with humans on a biological level in traditions that span the globe. Ms. Ortega was 12 years old at the time and living in New York City when this tall, blond, green-eyed entity suddenly materialized in her bedroom.

"At first, I saw two lights. I felt a presence, and naturally felt scared. One light was red in color and the other was green," she recalled. The lights told her not to fear for her safety. As she began to fall asleep, in spite of the luminous globes' presence, she felt caresses and kisses all over her body as her nightclothes were removed. "I felt something spread my legs open and a sharp pain soon after. I woke up, terrified, and saw a being in a tight-fitting outfit in bed with me. His eyes were so green that it made me dizzy to look at them. I found him very handsome, was attracted to him and fell in love."

Monica's lover and his silent companion (never manifested in human form) told her that they traveled around the world. Curiosity, they advised her, was the motivation for their sexual contacts.

In 1987, Monica had her third contact with the Watchers. After two years, she had moved back to Colombia, and was overjoyed at seeing her otherworldly lover again. At the end of their encounter, Monica expressed a desire to go with him to "his world," but the being turned her down. Nineteen years old at the time of the interview, the young woman had still not had sex with a human male. "They have the advantage," she explained, meaning the Watchers, "of not making you pregnant."

A History of the Watchers

The mystical figure of Apollonius of Tyana-sorcerer, philosopher and indefatigable traveler-visited a place, according to the chronicles, known as the City of the Gods, whose inhabitants allegedly "lived on the earth, yet outside it at the same time." Said parallel universe or dimension was located in the Himalayas, and as Apollonius and his guide, Damis, would near their destination, the more unreal the landscape became. Apollonius' larger-than-life adventures include teleportation away from the court of the Emperor Domitian in AD 96, and other occult phenomena.

Could these skills have been learned in the City of the Gods? Considering Apollonius' stature in ancient history, could he himself have been a Watcher?

Metal disks have been reported in the skies over the Himalayas for centuries. These have been considered manifestations of the Watchers by the lamas of Tibet and Nepal—"a sign of Shamballah," the subterranean (or extradimensional) land ruled by a higher order of beings who visit our world in gleaming metallic vehicles. Foremost among Shamballah's denizens is the Rigden-Jye-Po, the King of the World, who is identified with the leader of the Sons of Light mentioned in the Dead Sea Scrolls.

The Scriptures Speak

To the dismay of those who expect hard-boiled facts every time, the vast majority of the literature concerning the Watchers lies in mythology and in religious documents such as the Old Testament.

In the Apocryphal book which bears his name, the Old Testament figure Enoch is taken to heaven to intercede on behalf of the fallen Watchers with the angels of the highest heavens. The appeal is turned down: for having taught the secrets of nature to human females, and worse yet, for having conceived children with human females (the giant Nephilim), the 200 spirits involved are condemned to never again regain their lofty status.

We are given the names of the ringleaders of this heavenly conspiracy, and one of them, in particular, does more than ring a bell to a ufologically minded ear: Semyaz. While phonetic similarity proves nothing, it is unusual that the leader of the alleged Pleiadans visiting Billy Meier at his Swiss retreat should call herself Semjase. Meier's claims have been at the center of a number of disputes, mainly accusations of fraud concerning the fantastic UFO photographs he circulated.

What evidence suggests that the Watchers mentioned by the ancient religious chronicles, and the entities that accompany the UFO phenomenon, are one and the same? A careful examination of certain contemporary cases, along with some outstanding ancient ones, can leave no doubt as to the conflict between the fallen Watchers (the 200 which descended in the ancient Middle East, led by Semyaz/Semjase), the "Forces of Good," and hapless mortal humans, stuck squarely in the middle.

Quetzalcoatl—Watcher in the New World?

"But life had need of an intelligence to embrace the universe. We cannot provide it, said the Old Ones. It has never had it, said the Earth Spirit. Man was little more than an empty, soulless bhuta … it was thus that Venus sent the mightiest being of the planet, Sanat Kumara, the Fire Lord, who descended upon Earth escorted by four great lords and a hundred attendants."

An author risks ridicule by employing a quote from Madame Blavatsky's *Book of Dzyan*, one of the mainstays of Theosophy, and allegedly one of mankind's "forbidden books." It is nevertheless an acceptable risk when dealing with the widespread notion that at some point in human prehistory (or "primohistory," as author Robert Charroux termed it), entities from other worlds, whether spiritual or physical, descended upon the earth on a civilizing mission.

The Venusian lord Sanat Kumara and his retinue allegedly instructed primitive man in the skills of agriculture and beekeeping, much in the same way that Semjaz's crew of Watchers went about the business of teaching the rudiments of civilization to the ever-attractive "daughters of men."

The Mesoamerican traditions of Ce-Acatl-Topiltzin-Quetzalcoatl, "Our Noble Prince Feathered Serpent," whose link to the planet Venus is paramount throughout Aztec legend, represent another surprising corollary to the tutelary presence of the Biblical Watchers. Two versions of the Quetzalcoatl legend have survived to our times. The most familiar deals with the fall of the god-king who was deceived into having sexual intercourse with his sister (shades of Arthurian legend). In repentance, he built his own funeral pyre and apotheotically returned to the planet Venus. Using his "magic mirror" of pure obsidian, Tezcatlipoca showed Quetzalcoatl his reflection—that of a wizened old man with a skull-like face. Recoiling in horror, the god hid himself until his enemy lured him out again, intoxicating him with wine and leading him to his downfall.

The second version involves the timeless, titanic struggle between Tezcatlipoca (embodiment of the physical world) and Quetzalcoatl (representing the mind and spirit). Quetzalcoatl is a truly protean figure—a teacher, master of esoteric lore, a demiurge in a world gripped by awesome forces, giver of laws and civilization.

It is little wonder that so many Mexican rulers and high priests assumed the culture god's name, causing much confusion to archaeologists and historians of later centuries. There was even an order of priests named Quetzalcoatl, whose semi-monastic rule (predating Christian monasteries) urged them to emulate the kindness and holiness of the Feathered Serpent in every way.

All ancient records agree that Quetzalcoatl made the discovery that maize was suitable nourishment for his human subjects. This fact is a troubling one for modern scholars, since the cultivation of maize goes back some 9,000 to 10,000 years. Admitting the existence of a great civilizing force such as this so far into the past upsets the historical tables to no end, so this information is safely relegated into the realm of myth.

"Quetzalcoatl the Man"—to differentiate him from the deity—has been identified in recent times with an Irish monk, a Viking warrior, the Apostle Thomas, a Grand Master of the Knights Templar, and myriad other identities. But all evidence points toward an initial man or superman of that name existing nearly 10,000 years ago, at the very dawn of the Neolithic Age. His existence has been entwined with the mystery of timeless pyramids of Teotihuacan. This connection, coupled with the sheer antiquity of the site, have led some authors to make the fantastic claim that the "feathered serpent" emblem found at the Temple of Quetzalcoatl in Teotihuacan represents no modern reptile, but the head of a dinosaur millions of years old.

Benign, Malevolent, or Both?

Although "scientific" ufology cringes at the mention of any angelic/demonic involvement, the recent spate of abductions engulfing the world provides cases that could be seen within such a context. Abduction researcher Barbara Bartholic has singled out a case in which a youth faced what at first appeared to be a "Nordic" type of male alien who reverted into a reptilian form, assaulting the unsuspecting young man and leaving furrows across his back.

While this sobering incident is presented in the light of the shapeshifting ability of a particular alien race, it is strongly reminiscent of texts of a religious nature that state that demons can sometimes appear as "angels of light," which is what the tall, blond alien visitors have been associated with.

The dichotomy over whether the Watchers are benign or evil has been approached with the same caution reserved for the "good angel/bad angel" case. As in the fragment from the Testament of Amram, we can see the existence of two very different kinds of Watcher. Some yogis, for instance, believe that the Dark Angels have been confined to certain dimensions. Renaissance authors wrote of the nine-day-long fall of the vanquished angels into Hell, based upon Greek legends of the casting of the Cyclops into Tartaros—so distant that an anvil would take nine days to hit bottom. Could there be a connection between the negative order of beings and the allegedly extraterrestrial visitors we are entertaining today?

In 1947, one Señor C.A.V. encountered strange amoeba-like beings in the desert outside Lima, Peru, who took him aboard their landed vehicle. The conversation between the stunned Señor C.A.V. and his nonhuman hosts turned to spiritual matters. They replied mockingly to his question about God, stating: "We are like Gods." Either the beings had a very high opinion of themselves, or they ranked among the fallen Watchers.

In the Kwa Sizabantu mission station in South Africa, a woman approached German theologian Kurt Koch to confess a strange encounter in the Namib Desert with a robot-crewed UFO. In the course of a telepathic conversation with the mechanical aliens, one of them declared: "God is not going to answer your prayers anyway. But we can fulfill your wishes."

More stories abound with regard to the benevolent Watchers, both in antiquity and in the present. A truly bewildering case of Watcher intervention into human life is submitted by Spanish UFO researcher Salvador Freixedo in his book *Ellos: Los Dueños Invisibles de este Mundo*. When a brush fire broke out on the estate of Colombian journalist Inés de Montaña, farmhands ran to and fro trying to create fire breaks in the middle of the night. Enormous tongues of flame lapped at the black skies while the journalist and her trusted housekeeper, Jovita Caicedo, looked on in sheer terror.

The old wooden farmhouse from which they beheld the breeze was about to be incinerated when "a helicopter of light," as de Montaña describes it, swooped in from the western sky. The coruscant light came closer, as low as the tops of the coconut palms, leaving a wake like a comet's tail in its path. It then began to emit a blast of intense cold, which had the effect of extinguishing the raging fire, dousing it as effectively as would have tons of water.

Montaña's incredible story was devoted an entire page in the newspaper for which she worked. "What you have read is the truth, supported by the testimony of four people who felt the effects of a strange phenomenon, and by the fact that in over 30 years, no one has been able to say that there has been fantasy, fiction or deceit in the thousands of words I've written," she stated.

Frank Smythe, a mountain climber ascending one of the Himalayan peaks, allegedly observed a "pulsating tea kettle" which seemed to be monitoring his progress. Smythe noted that before seeing it, he'd had the sensation of someone benignly watching his efforts.

It has been suggested that what we are seeing is "police activity" of a sort on the behalf of the positive Watchers, as they go about their appointed rounds, fending off the attacks of the renegade contingent. While some may find this hard to accept, some confirmation can be found in events that took place in Spain during a very heavy period of UFO activity in that country in the early 1980s.

The town of Isla Cristina, on Spain's southern coast, was plagued by UFOs, giant creatures thrashing across the tidal swamps, and a host of other hair-raising and disturbing phenomena. María Echague, a resident of the town, witnessed two tall, slender, white-haired figures who appeared to move in unison some 40 meters from where she stood. Amazed by the odd beauty and synchronicity of movement displayed by the beings, Ms. Echague found herself thinking *Que sois?* ("What are you?") The beings turned in unison to show her the raised thumb, index and middle fingers of their right hands (a classic esoteric gesture, symbolizing the triumph of spirit over matter) and mentally replied: "We are teachers," before disappearing.

The Watchers continue to stage spectaculars for the benefit of those whom they contact and the spellbound followers of these "modern prophets" as well. Augusta de Almeidda, a contactee from the Philippines, was advised by her "alien brothers" that an aerial display of their majesty would take place over an arena on June 12, 1992. Four hundred onlookers witnessed golden spherical and cigar-shaped vehicles of varied geometry over the stadium at 8:05 that evening.

Conclusion

Talk of supernatural Watchers—"Sons of God" who mated with human females at the dawn of time and were cast out from their lofty position by divine powers—tends to annoy the believer in extraterrestrial visitors and/or ancient astronauts. But it would be both unrealistic and unwise to discount the strong paranormal component that exists in the UFO phenomenon. Some expressions of this phenomenon echo the persistent notion of a primeval struggle between good and evil factions that is at the root of many different mythologies—the clash between Ormuzd and Ahriman in Zoroastrianism, that between Ouranos and the Cyclops in Greek myth, the struggle between Bacaab-Quich, and Tohil in the Mayan cosmology, and the struggle between Quetzalcoatl and Tezcatlipoca.

As Amram cautioned his children in his testament: "I leave you my books in testimony, that you might be warned by them … "

Broomsticks, Shamans, and UFOs
By Nigel Watson
November–December 2008

Editors' note: The term "witchcraft" in this article refers to distorted popular beliefs rather than Wiccan or Pagan practice.

The assault and abduction of men and women is not restricted to the brightly lit chambers of flying saucers inhabited by the cold, calculating, Grey alien tormentors. Visions, UFOs, entities, magical flights, Men in Black, time loss, vehicle stoppages, abductions, implants, invisibility, sexual intercourse, and hybrid offspring are just some of the features of witchcraft and shamanism.

Witchcraft

For centuries, the belief that witchcraft was being used to commune with the devil and his minions from hell was prevalent throughout Europe, culminating in the witchcraft craze that raged from the 1400s to the 1600s. Witches were thought to possess supernatural powers, including the ability to damage crops and to kill or spread illness to livestock and humans.

In the small Lincolnshire village of Revesby, England, six miles south of Horncastle, an ancient burial marked by two 100-foot diameter tumuli was thought to be the location for the witches' sabbath. On the night of a full moon, hundreds of witches from far and wide would allegedly smear themselves with ointment and fly astride a broomstick to this location. Leaving storm and destruction in their wake, they would see the devil appear before them. He would take on all manner of horrifying guises, from lion or bear to hydra-headed monster. After worship and sacrifices, each witch would tell of the famines and plagues they had spread and the unbaptized children and weak Christians they had put in the service of Satan. Finally, there would be dancing, feasting, and drunken orgies.

The people of Revesby kept well away, but one day in 1632 a stranger visited the village and became beguiled by their stories of the nearby sabbath. That night this captain of His Majesty's bodyguard decided to see it for himself.

In the glow of the full moon, he approached the tumuli where he heard a weird cry that sent him into a nervous sweat. His legs seemed to force him to walk over the hill. At the top he looked down to see about a hundred half-naked women and girls dancing around a stone altar that was still burning from some sacrifice to Satan. The chanting women, sensing his presence, swooped on him like a flock of vultures. He felt their sharp claws, then he was sent flying through the air before he lost consciousness.

He woke the next morning outside the Sun Inn, covered in wounds as if he had been attacked by a giant bird. He was in a critical state for many days. On recovering, he returned immediately to London.

Stories like this may have arisen to stop strangers and authorities from probing illegal gatherings, or used as entertainment to scare the gullible. Nonetheless, the detail that the captain felt compelled to walk toward the sabbath is reminiscent of stories told by UFO witnesses who cannot resist meeting aliens or going inside their craft despite their conscious desire not to. The sensation of flying, the injuries, and the association of these events with an ancient site are also consistent with reports found in UFO literature.

Sometimes witches were accused of abducting people to join in their unpleasant activities. In the 1692 Salem witch trials, Susanna Martin was accused of flying farmer Joseph Ring from his bed to black sabbaths on a regular basis for two years. Every time he was returned home, he was struck dumb, making it impossible for him to tell anyone what had happened. Through the agency of God, rather than hypnosis, he was able to recount his experiences to the trial.

Men in Black

The main ingredient of the witches' flying ointment was often thought to be the boiled fat of unbaptized infants. In 1664, a group of Somerset witches was put on trial, during which they confessed that they were given a greenish-colored ointment by a mysterious man dressed in black.

Accused witch Elisabeth Style said that after rubbing the ointment on their bodies they called out, "Tout, tout a tout, tout, throughout and about to fly," to take flight, and to return they called, "Rentum Tormentum."

This story indicates that mysterious men in black appeared long before they became notorious in UFO literature. Hilary Evans notes that they are featured in the folklore and legends of most countries. Most of the time they are associated with the works of the devil, as in the case of a young lad who confessed to a French court on June 2, 1603, that he was forced to carry out tasks for a tall, dark man dressed in black. These acts included kidnapping a child and eating him.

During the Welsh religious revival of 1904 to 1905, one of the leaders of the movement, Mary Jones, frequently saw lights that appeared to be under intelligent control. These lights were often seen over the homes of those who were about to convert. On three occasions, a man in black appeared in her bedroom and gave her a message she was forbidden to pass on. One MIB visitation was terminated when a ball of light shot a ray of white light at it. Jones also had out-of-body experiences, visions, and other paranormal events surrounding her, much like a modern-day abductee.

A 13-year-old girl was trimming a hat one Saturday night in the early 1900s when, "As the clock struck twelve, the front door opened, then the parlor door, and a man entered and sat down in a chair opposite to me. He was rather short, very thin, dressed in black, with an extremely pale face, and hands with very long thin fingers. He had a high silk hat on his head, and in one hand he held an old-fashioned, large silver snuffbox. He gazed at me and said three times, slowly and distinctly, 'I've come to tell you.' He then vanished, and I noted that the door was shut as before."

A visitor was given the same room to sleep in two years later. He knew nothing of the girl's story, yet at the stroke of midnight he had the same vision. The man in black was explained as the spirit of a dead person. When the house was demolished, this idea seemed to be confirmed, as a skeleton holding a snuffbox was found buried underneath this room.

Succubi and Incubi

Female demons called *succubi* were believed to come at night to indulge in sexual intercourse with men. Male demons called *incubi* allegedly visited women for the same purpose. Hundreds of men and women claimed such unions; their stories are similar to those of the victims of the sex-crazed alien abductors of today.

Vehicle stoppages were long associated with witches. In Lincolnshire, it was believed that a witch could stop a team of horses without saying a word, and they would not move until she wanted them to.

There are accounts of people on bicycles being influenced by outside forces. In 1918, two young men were cycling home to Listowel, Ireland, when they both felt a strange force holding them back. Although the road was level, they had trouble making any progress and their tongues seemed to be paralyzed.

In Lincolnshire again, around 1925, a cyclist was going to Legbourne when his front light went out. After he re-lit his acetylene lamp, the rear light went out. He re-lit the rear light and was just about to ride away when both lights went out. Once he had the lights going again he rode away as quickly as possible.

Both of these events took place where there had been violent murders. The latter was also associated with ghostly events and a persistent mist. These happenings precede reports that UFO force fields can stop cars and disrupt electronic equipment.

The connection between abductions and witchcraft beliefs is made explicit in the story of 34-year-old "Joe," who believed the aliens had an interest in him from before his birth. They took sperm from him mechanically and presented him with his own offspring. As a child, Joe had a recurring nightmare about a witch comparable to the Wicked Witch of the West in *The Wizard of Oz*. The witch would fly through his bedroom window and with her huge, staring eyes hypnotize him to climb onto her broomstick. Powerless to resist, he would be flown away. These nightmares made him afraid to go to sleep for fear of being abducted.

Shamans and Alien Contact

Abductees have also been compared to shamans, who in most cultures commune with the spirits of the dead and gain their mystical knowledge through tortuous initiation and ritual. Shamanic experiences have several parallels with abduction accounts, including capture, initiation, magical flights involving meetings with spirits, and return to our world.

A person can become a shaman through training and guidance or by accident through the intervention of dreams, visions, or even psychological problems. Mircea Eliade, in *Shamanism: Archaic Techniques of Ecstasy*, noted: "A man or woman may be made a seer by being bodily abducted by the spirits. [A young man] was taken up to heaven by the sky spirits and given a beautiful body such as theirs. When he returned to earth, he was a seer and the sky-spirits served him in his cures."

Shamanic initiation for Australian aborigines involved being stabbed in the head, thereby allowing a magical stone to be placed inside the wound by a supernatural being. Lights were also associated with the shamanic experience, which could involve the shaman's head being filled with light. Tiny balls of light have been seen surrounding shamans. These lights can cause electronic equipment to go haywire.

Bright flames and luminous clouds have also been regarded as shamanic spirits.

Initiations usually involved the ritualistic dismemberment of the body so that the initiate is able to confront his own mortality and return as a spiritually enlightened magician. Anthropologists Walter Baldwin Spencer and Francis James Gillen, in *The Northern Tribes of Central Australia* (1904), described the initiation of an aborigine called Kurkutji, who was confronted in a cave by spirits named Mundadji and Munkaninji:

"Mundadji cut him open, right down the middle line, took out all of his insides and exchanged them for those of himself, which he placed in the body of Kurkutji. At the same time he put a number of sacred stones in his body. After it was all over, the youngest spirit, Munkaninji, came up and restored him to life, told him that he was now a medicine-man and showed him how to extract bones and other forms of evil magic out of them. Then he took him away up into the sky and brought him down to earth close to his own camp, where he heard the natives mourning for him, thinking that he was dead. For a long time he remained in a more or less dazed condition, but gradually he recovered and the natives knew that he had been made into a medicine man. When he operates, the spirit Munkaninji is supposed to be near at hand watching him, unseen of course by ordinary people."

Extreme Operations

This brings to mind the abduction experiences of Sandra Larson, who said her brain was removed. It also relates to the case of Martin Bolton, who thought that aliens had put a communication device inside his head in 1979. He experienced extreme pain from evil aliens who used ray guns on his head and knee joints, poured chemicals on his head, stretched his penis, doctored his intestines, gave him phantom pregnancies, infected him with influenza germs, and caused him to vomit.

Dr. Daniel Paul Schreber, an appeals court judge, was kept in various German asylums between 1893 and 1902. He believed that he had suffered plague and died, and his body had decomposed. His stomach, intestines, and lungs were removed and eventually returned by divine miracle "rays." He also thought that God was turning him into a woman so that he could give birth to a new race of men who would achieve bliss.

In other cultures and times, rather than psychiatric cases, these men might well have been regarded as shamans.

In 1980, about the time Bolton was having his experiences, Nevill Drury took a shamanic journey. He traveled through tunnels, encountered saintly figures, saw phoenix images, had a crystal implanted in his chest, and viewed a crystal palace, all of which led him to his inner being. Similar elements were also present in Betty Andreasson's UFO experiences.

Shamanic spirits, like UFO entities, come in all shapes and sizes: beautiful women; horned, foul things; little men with bald, pointed heads; and living dolls. Animals, especially deer but also birds, wolves, and bears, are regarded as guides and helpers to the shaman. These are reminiscent of the animals seen by abductees that are explained as screen memories.

Shamans, like contactees, can marry and have children with their spirits. One account told of a female shaman who had a child from such a union. At night while her family slept, as if "dead," the spirit father came with the baby so that she could breast-feed it. Again, this reminds us of the presentation of hybrid babies to abductees.

Healing and Enlightenment

Shamans are attributed with healing powers that employ such techniques as dream interpretation, counseling, and psychodrama. The experiences recounted by abductees to John Mack do seem to take people on a spiritual journey like those of the shaman. The experience of "Dave" involved the humiliation of having a long flexible instrument inserted into his rectum, an implant put in his stomach, and sperm taken from him. He believed that, in a previous incarnation, he was a Native American boy who met his spirit guide, an alien named Velia, at the top of Pemsit Mountain. Dave had a strong association with natural forces, and Velia seems to have guided him through several lifetimes.

Whitley Strieber has speculated that the symbols and language of shamanism came about in the past due to our interaction with alien visitors. Shamanic-type experiences and spiritual enlightenment are increasingly being sought by obtaining contact with alien entities or forces.

Lyssa Royal, a channeler who grew up in New Hampshire, often heard her family often talk about Betty and Barney Hill's alien abduction experience. She and her family saw a UFO in 1979 when she was 18 years old. At college, she studied psychology and learned how to induce self-hypnosis.

When Royal graduated, she met a channeler called Darryl Anka. He was in contact with an extraterrestrial entity called Bashar. Royal made her own extraterrestrial contacts to learn about human history and for the purpose of self-improvement. She has written several books about her contacts with aliens, including *Visitors from Within* and *Preparing for Contact*. In the 1990s, she became involved with the Center for the Study of Extraterrestrial Intelligence (CSETI), which attempted to make contact with aliens. They claimed that they saw structured craft result from their efforts to make contact.

The alien abduction experience seems to have several links and comparisons with witchcraft and shamanism, leaving us to ponder whether aliens have plagued us through the centuries in a variety of grotesque guises or whether these experiences and stories are intrinsically human: self-generated psychological and cultural phenomena.

UFOs: 3-D or 4-D+
By Karl T. Pflock and James W. Moseley

September 2000

What are UFOs? Where do they come from? Why are they here? What do their operators want? These questions have bedeviled ufologists for more than half a century, and appear little closer to being answered objectively and definitively today than they were when they were first asked.

But this does not preclude informed speculation.

Jim Moseley and I have quite different ideas about what the answers may be, and to some degree even what the real questions are. In a nutshell—or, rather, two nutshells—here is what we think. Jim gets the first word.

UFOs—According to Moseley

Throughout recorded history, there have been events of all kinds that do not fit into the proper scheme of things—astronomical apparitions, hauntings, poltergeists, unexplainable coincidences, and, of course, things seen in the sky that should not be there. The champion chronicler of such matters was the late, great Charles Fort, and I am proud to consider myself one of his followers. Fort did not seriously attempt to explain these anomalies. He just threw them in the face of Science and in effect said, "Here. Explain this!"

Some of these weird happenings are easily explainable with a proper knowledge of science and by discarding obviously unprovable superstitions. Others defy explanation, unless one assumes they are products of delusion, mistake, or hoaxing. On the other hand, there rarely is any physical proof to back up these startling claims. Thus, True Believers have a valid excuse for believing, while True Unbelievers have an equally good excuse for disbelieving.

It all depends on your starting point. Objectivity, even with the best of intentions, is almost impossible to come by.

There was a time when the conventional wisdom was that the sun revolves around the earth. Science has since shown us that earth is merely one of several planets revolving about a not particularly important star, just one of countless others in this huge and extremely peculiar universe.

Yet mankind insists on feeling important. The latest ego trip is to believe we are so important that intelligent beings have come across the void just to study us. This makes us very important indeed!

I share the view that life is common in the universe, and that, yes, it sometimes has evolved to become what we would call intelligent. I even accept the idea that, if there were intelligent beings somewhere that just happen to be in what I call the exploring stage, and if they had the motivation and technical means, they might come here. But that is an awful lot of "ifs." I will even grant that the speed-of-light limit could be overcome by a highly technical civilization.

So let us assume "they" could get here if they really wanted to. But I still wonder: Why would they want to? (It has been said there is no life on Mars—except on Saturday night.)

Now compound these improbabilities with another: Our Visitors just happen to look almost exactly like us. Note that most are shorter than us, which is very important. As a race, we are still so primitive that we are less afraid of "little men" (gray, green, or otherwise) than we would be, say, of 20-footers—who theoretically are just as likely as the little guys.

Most of the Visitors who do not fit the little-men category fall into the Benevolent Space Beings box. Here we have Orthon and all the wonderful beings whom contactees of old used to hobnob with. They were full of feel-good philosophy, though they quite literally never told us anything specific that we did not already know. There were no scientific formulas, no precisely accurate predictions, no clear prescriptions for better human relations. Just drivel.

Then there is the problem of no coherent Visitor agenda. The Visitors act in ways that seem arbitrary, meaningless, and sometimes just plain stupid. They are obsessed with sex—as we are—and worst of all, they allegedly impregnate human women, conceiving hybrid babies, something even closely related earth species cannot do. They leave "implants" in the bodies of selected humans, and yet no one has learned why. They perform the same sort of sexual-medical manipulations with humans over and over again, obsessively.

There probably is some sort of truth behind some of this weirdness. But rather than looking to space beings, it seems much more likely to me that we are dealing with an intelligence that is and always has been a permanent four- or extra-dimensional (4-D+) part of the Earth's environment.

Another problem with the idea of space visitors is that earthly evolution has been going on for hundreds of millions of years. Only in the past 5,000 to 10,000 years have we achieved anything resembling civilization. What will we be like if we keep advancing and evolving at the same pace for another million years, or even just a thousand? The results are literally unimaginable.

In 1,000 years, I doubt we will be bothering to go off looking for similar civilizations in space. We will be way beyond that stage, into whatever follows. Today, we are in the exploring stage and may remain so for a couple of hundred more years. Are we interacting with another three-dimensional (3-D) civilization that just happens to be in the same stage? The odds are overwhelmingly against it.

Would a highly advanced civilization be doing what we are doing? I think not. It seems to me that a supremely evolved race would, in effect, be just one entity, with total knowledge, living in a perpetual state of ecstasy—God, if you like. Such an entity would not be running about looking for primitive creatures like us. It would have no need, no motivation to go anywhere. It would already be "there."

If we insist on believing creatures from other planets are visiting us, we must admit that much of what they do represents "magic," activity beyond our level of comprehension. We can call them advanced beings we do not understand, or 4-D, or whatever we want. The simple fact is, we natives are very primitive, and our Visitors—if any—simply are beyond present understanding.

It is not unreasonable to assume that among the "magic" being practiced upon us are ways of interacting with the human mind. Thus, it is unreasonable to separate "nuts and bolts" UFOs and their occupants from astral entities, philosophical space brothers, poltergeists, Ouija board spirits, et cetera. All are part of the same spectrum of phenomena, all to one degree or another beyond our present knowledge.

We humans do not like to admit anything is beyond the grasp of our minds. So when there are no reasonable answers, we make up something. Better to believe the absurd than to admit ignorance. Yet scientists (theoretically) have learned to say, "We don't know the answer to that," and live with it. They often add, "But we'll know someday." This is an article of faith, which may be true. Meanwhile, 4-D+ reality continues to intrude and we keep making up answers.

UFOs—According to Pflock

A major stumbling block to cracking the UFO mystery is what J. Allen Hynek called the "embarrassment of riches." We are confronted with an incredible array of disparate phenomena on which the label "UFO" has been hung. Call it a UFO, it is a UFO.

Thus some have come to mistake the label for the reality. If science approached its work the way proto-science ufology has, wombats and supernovas would be lumped together, undifferentiated and both about as well understood as UFOs and other anomalies are today. Just because someone thinks something is a UFO, or UFO-related, does not make it so.

The seeming connections between and among various paranormal phenomena and UFOs, and many of the particulars of what people report and how they characterize their experiences, seem to me to arise from two perfectly understandable human tendencies. Some are consequences of careless and wishful thinking. More arise from perfectly natural and honest, conscious and unconscious attempts to interpret extraordinary events in terms of ordinary experience.

To the degree anything paranormal (or seemingly so) is associated with reports of things that clearly are nuts-and-bolts vehicles and their quite substantial occupants, it is likely to stem from our present level of knowledge. As Sir Arthur Clarke has observed, any sufficiently advanced science and its resulting technology, would appear to us as magic. Which does not make it magic in any extra- or supernormal sense. It just looks that way because we lack a mental-experiential frame of reference to deal with it.

But we may not be all that far away from such understanding. Today, NASA is developing plasma-spike "disk ships" that bear an uncanny resemblance to the flying saucer captured in the famed McMinnville, Oregon, photographs of 1950. These craft will be capable of speeds up to 35,000 miles an hour within the atmosphere, without burning up or creating a sonic boom. In a U.S. Air Force laboratory just down the road from where I am writing this, scientists are experimenting with model "lightships," which make true right-angle turns and can both hover and accelerate faster than the human eye can follow, seeming to just disappear into and appear out of thin air. Is this beginning to sound like flying saucers to you? Then there are quantum computers, the recent announcement of new materials that cause certain laws of physics to run backward, the potential for tapping into "free" zero-point energy, and so on and on.

Today's paranormal phenomena may well be tomorrow's everyday technology—and may be so already for advanced civilizations on planets orbiting other stars.

Some suggest UFO beings are too much like us to be from another planet. However, it stands to reason that space-faring beings would seek out worlds similar to their own. As a consequence of evolutionary selection, odds are that such travelers would bear a passing resemblance to the locals—in this case, us. This dispute was amusingly summed up in a television talk-show exchange between astronomer-skeptic Carl Sagan and UFO abductee Betty Hill. Sagan said he would find elephant-like aliens more believable than humanoids. Mrs. Hill retorted, "If they looked like elephants, then they'd be bothering the elephants." My money is on Betty's assessment.

There are far too many credible UFO reports on record that are most simply and directly explained as encounters with extraterrestrial craft and beings to dismiss such an explanation in favor of a "unified field theory" of all things tagged UFO. If these forced bedfellows were instead carefully sorted out and independently subjected to rigorous study, relating them as such study suggests it is appropriate to do, we would be much more likely to understand what we are dealing with in all cases—nuts-and-bolts saucers and paranormal phenomena alike.

Based on the evidence, I am of the opinion that we have been visited by 3-D beings from an extra-solar planet of our galaxy. I think they came here because our sun and its planets seemed cozily familiar. They studied our entire system and us quite closely for 30 years or so.

Once in a while a couple of alien graduate students got out of hand and buzzed the natives. On occasion some ambitious scientists overstepped a bit and grabbed a human or two for study—as, for example, in the famous (and, in my opinion, very real) 1961 abduction of Betty and Barney Hill.

Then they moved on, leaving us wondering, dreaming, hoping, and more than a little confused. They may have left automatic monitors or even a small contingent of observers behind to keep an eye on things. If so, they probably will return and eventually make overt contact. It would behoove us to be ready when they do, to make their "magic" ours and meet them on as equal a footing as possible.

FIVE: You Make the Call

UFOs: 3-D, 4-D+, or something else entirely? We leave it to you to decide.

Some Recent Considerations

After all these years, we are still wondering and speculating about the true nature of UFOs. The prevailing opinion seems to remain, especially in the popular imagination, that they are extraterrestrial spacecraft piloted by little gray men with big eyes—the old pulp fiction concept of bug-eyed monsters, or BEMs. Personally, I feel that the truth cannot possibly be that simple, or that complicated. Meanwhile, sightings continue unabated, and so does the wonder and puzzlement. Here are a few articles from recent years that reflect contemporary 21st-century thinking on the subject and in some cases or offer new insight into old happenings.

Shadowcraft and the UFO Phenomenon
By Curt Sutherly

September 2003

On an autumn night in 1994, a motorist in Nova Scotia was en route to Halifax when she and her passenger encountered a dark, diamond-shaped flying object outlined by white lights. The object hovered silently over their vehicle before vanishing to the west. The incident was one of 186 UFO events reported to Canadian officials in 1994 and filed with the National Archives in Ottawa.

On October 16, 1998, a diamond-shaped UFO was observed over Edinburgh, Scotland. According to investigator Ron Halliday, the object was illuminated by "two bright white lights … and had a red light underneath." The UFO—flying low over Edinburgh's Corstorphine Hill—was spotted by an area woman who, Halliday said, "was going to bed about 11:30 p.m. when she saw the object from her window."

On August 28, 2001, about 9:30 p.m., a strange flying object was observed over the town of Walsall, England. The lone witness at first believed the object to be a large aircraft—perhaps a commercial airliner—because of its size. As it approached, however, he could see it was distinctly triangular in shape. It also made no sound. The UFO remained in sight for about ten minutes. Before vanishing from view it underwent a startling transformation: the object changed shape, shifting from its triangular form to that of a somewhat "flattened" diamond.

In the UFO realm, diamonds are a rarity—much more uncommon than flying discs, cigars, spheres, or even triangles (which until recent years were also quite uncommon). Interestingly enough, the diamond or faceted form has special significance in the murky realm of stealth aircraft technology—an area we will now examine, along with its intriguing—and perhaps inevitable—connection to the UFO realm.

The Shadowcraft

Modern stealth technology has the ability to render an aircraft nearly (but not entirely) invisible to radar. Combine this technology with experimental or prototype aircraft designs and propulsion systems, and the result is a "shadowcraft"—a name applied to any aircraft that the Defense Department denies knowledge of or insists does not exist.

In the United States, work to create stealth technology began in earnest during the mid-1970s. At that time, key elements of the aerospace industry were approached by the Pentagon's Defense Advanced Research Projects Agency to try and develop an "experimental survivable testbed"—an aircraft that would have a truly small "radar cross section" (a measure of how large an object appears on a radar screen), making it extremely difficult to detect.

One aerospace team initially excluded from the competition was the Lockheed "Skunk Works" in Palmdale, California—the shop that developed the now famous U-2 spyplane and the superfast SR-71 "Blackbird." For some in the industry, this was a surprising omission inasmuch as the SR-71—designed during the 1950s by Clarence L. ("Kelly") Johnson and Ben Rich, Johnson's chief engineer—was the first aircraft to incorporate rudimentary stealth technology into its design.

Despite being shut out, Rich managed to lever his way into the competition based on his team's earlier work. One crucial member of that team was Denys Overholser, a radar expert and mathematician who ran the Skunk Works computational group. He was known in aerospace circles as the "Wizard of Oz."

It wasn't long before Overholser stirred up controversy.

Using an early model Cray supercomputer, the mathematician developed, in only six weeks, a highly specialized computer program called ECHO-1. With this program— primitive by today's standards as it was based on old-style computer punch cards—Overholser's group was able to calculate the optimum shape needed to deflect or scatter radar in such a way as to greatly reduce the aircraft signature. That ideal shape was a faceted diamond.

When Overholser reported his findings to Lockheed engineers, he was greeted with skepticism. In fact, the engineers were so skeptical that they dubbed his idea the "Hopeless Diamond." Nonetheless, when rigorously compared to the best design the engineers had developed, Overholser's approach easily won out. Using an improved version of ECHO-1, and operating under the code name "Have Blue," his group produced a series of aircraft designs that ultimately led to the development of the F-117A "Nighthawk" stealth fighter with its faceted fuselage shape.

The Nighthawk

With a length of nearly 66 feet and a wingspan of 43 feet, the Nighthawk appears on radar to be about the size of a sea gull. To better understand how impressively small this is, consider that a single 1950s era B-52 bomber has a radar cross section that is larger than all of the F-117s built for combat—a total of 59 aircraft!

Cloaked in a veil of intense secrecy, the first of the F-117s were declared operationally ready in October 1983. Around the same time, a series of dramatic UFO events was gaining momentum in New York's Hudson River Valley. The UFO sightings began in late 1982 and continued nearly unabated well into the 1990s. Residents of the valley observed, and sometimes videotaped, large, often brightly illuminated triangular and boomerang-shaped flying objects that moved silently—and sometimes quite slowly—across the night sky.

In November 1988, the Air Force unveiled the B-2 Stealth bomber, a manta-ray-shaped flying wing. Skeptics, and those not familiar with the complexity of the UFO phenomenon, concluded that the mysterious objects reported in New York and elsewhere were secret night tests of the B-2. This speculation abounded despite the fact that the B-2 made its maiden flight on July 17, 1989—months after its unveiling and more than seven years after the earliest reports in the Hudson Valley. Skeptics also suggested that the F-117 was responsible for some of the mysterious sightings.

Unfortunately, neither the B-2 nor the F-117A has the capability to fly at extremely slow speeds or in total silence. They are "stealthy" only in the sense that they are dark in color and largely invisible to radar at a distance. The objects observed in the Hudson Valley often moved so slowly that, were they conventional aircraft, they would have stalled and fallen out of the sky.

The appearance of slow moving, brightly illuminated UFOs over heavily populated areas is not consistent with the testing of top-secret aircraft. In fact, it suggests quite the opposite: that someone or something wants to be seen! There are other problems as well, such as the oft-reported ability of UFOs to disappear or "blink out" and almost immediately reappear somewhere else, or to speed away at what is clearly a supersonic pace, and do either of these things without triggering a sonic boom (which means they do not displace air).

In addition, there is the matter of shapeshifting UFOs, such as described earlier. This is a phenomenon that has long been a part of the UFO puzzle and which has grown increasingly prevalent in recent years. There is no easy explanation for this (unless one wants to assume that the eyewitnesses are all completely off their rocker, which is certainly not the case). Indeed, the technology needed to enable an aircraft to change physical form or to disappear and reappear in an instant would have to be based on something like quantum mechanics and not on classical physics, and at our present level of science this puts us—for all intents and purposes—into the realm of magic.

Triangular UFOs

Another UFO mystery that has arisen in recent years—one that might involve shadowcraft—has to do with reports of a fairly specific type of triangular or deltoid-shaped object observed in widespread locations. These reports differ from most UFO events (including most reports of triangular UFOs) in that they tend to be of solitary low-lit or non-illuminated (as opposed to brightly illuminated) objects observed late at night—a purely accidental sighting, or so it would seem.

Consider the following account:

About 1:00 a.m. on November 18, 1999, an individual approximately one mile west of Ohio State University spotted a dark flying object in the shape of an equilateral triangle. About 1:50 a.m., a suburban Columbus, Ohio, police officer, and a reserve officer for a different department riding with the first officer, spotted the same object or one virtually identical to it. The object was visible for 5 to 15 seconds and was initially observed moving east to west. The officers, who exited their cruiser for a better view, said the UFO was silent and made a slow banking turn to the right. As it did so a dark underside was revealed, devoid of lights but distorted as if somehow camouflaged.

The object—close enough to the witnesses so that sharp, defined edges could be seen despite the distortion and lack of illumination—completed a 90-degree turn to the north while banking and then leveled off. The suburban Columbus officer said the object seemed to glide though the air much as stingray glides through the water. The object was described as large—much larger than a police helicopter—and also moved more slowly than the average speed of a helicopter. A check by the officer with personnel at Port

Columbus Airport revealed that nothing unusual had been detected on radar.

So what was this object? A possible explanation appeared in the September 1999 issue of *Popular Mechanics*.

In that issue, science editor Jim Wilson details the curious history of the Lockheed-Martin Skunk Works. Near the end of the article, Wilson mentions the possibility that a "stealth blimp" may have been built by the Skunk Works. The blimp, he said, "supposedly carries a massive phased array radar. The craft is said to disguise itself by using 'optical stealth' technology [emphasis added] that creates an image of a floating star field."

Wilson's article triggered rampant speculation among UFO aficionados: Was it possible that a blimp, of all things, was responsible for some of the sightings of huge triangular or deltoid-shaped UFOs?

Actually, yes!

Proposals for near-neutral buoyancy, rigid-bodied (as opposed to soft-bodied) high-tech craft are well documented in aviation circles, going back to at least the mid-1960s. In fact, in August 1970 a 26-foot-long working prototype of just such a craft was flown by the Aereon Corporation of Princeton, New Jersey. In the mid-1990s, Aereon obtained preliminary government funding to build a lighter-than-air lifting body that could contain a number of large radar antennae. Aereon officials claim the craft was never built—at least not by them. But that doesn't mean someone else didn't build it.

Assuming someone else did build a stealth blimp, it would explain some—though certainly not all—of the more intriguing reports of strange triangular craft.

The Aurora

In 1993, the Testor Corporation of Rockford, Illinois—a leading manufacturer of model airplanes—unveiled a new model called the "Aurora," representing the long-rumored replacement for the SR-71 Blackbird. The designer was aviation writer-historian John Andrews, who in the late 1950s created an accurate model of the then top-secret U-2 spy plane. In 1986, Andrews created a model version of the F-117A stealth fighter (his design was not entirely accurate but he was clearly on the right track), prompting strong denials from the Defense Department about the existence of any such craft. In 1993, his "Aurora" model provoked similar strong denials.

The Testor Aurora was a two-stage design: a black, triangular craft attached to a much larger SR-71 style lifting body. At full scale, Andrews estimated that the larger aircraft would measure about 160 feet in length, and the triangular vehicle about 80 feet.

On August 4, 1999, a number of individuals were gathered in the parking lot of the Pickwick Market and Gas facility, just south of the Little A'Le'Inn restaurant in the town of Rachel, Nevada. The town is located in the high desert along State Highway 375, northwest of Las Vegas, and not far (as the crow flies) from the government facility at Groom Dry Lake, otherwise known as Area 51.

According to a report in the March 2000 *MUFON UFO Journal*, the individuals in the parking lot heard the sound of an approaching T-38 jet trainer. The time was about 10:30 a.m. The T-38 was not alone. According to the report, the trainer was flying support for a much larger, black, arrow-shaped aircraft. The mystery plane flew silently and slowly, "giving ... the impression that it was cooling its engines in preparation for a landing at Area 51," the report stated. The length of the aircraft was estimated at between 150 and 180 feet—a length that compares quite favorably with the 160-foot scale length for the Aurora lifting body designed by John Andrews!

This account, if accurate, would seem to be a clear indication that someone is operating a new supersecret plane. Moreover, it is substantiated by other reports of this type, including a 1989 sighting over the North Sea by a qualified British aircraft observer. That sighting was of a large black triangle flying directly astern a KC-135 tanker aircraft, with two F-111 fighter-bombers flying escort.

Aviation insiders believe reports such as these are sightings of a replacement for the SR-71, which was retired by the Air Force in 1990 and then reactivated briefly before being permanently retired in 1997. They may be correct.

While operational, the Blackbird required a special hydrocarbon fuel known as JP-7. The fuel had a low flash point and a two-week shelf life, and had to be safely disposed of beyond that time. A fleet of specially modified KC-135 tanker aircraft carried JP-7 for inflight refueling of the SR-71. According to sources within the aerospace community, as of early 2000, JP-7 was still being made and the specialized KC-135 tankers were still in service. Clearly, some aircraft other than the SR-71 has been using this unique fuel!

Some aviation enthusiasts might speculate that a recently unveiled aircraft known as the "Bird of Prey" has been using this special SR-71 fuel. The Bird of Prey—named after the Klingon spacecraft on Star Trek—is a radically designed single-seat stealth prototype that was built at Boeing Aircraft's top-secret Phantom Works in California (Boeing's counterpart to the Lockheed-Martin Skunk Works). The prototype successfully flew 38 times between 1996 and 1999, the duration of the program, and was unveiled publicly last October.

Unlike other stealth aircraft, which fly only at night, the Bird of Prey can operate in the day, utilizing what Boeing and the Air Force refer to only as "new low-observable technologies." Unofficially, the aircraft probably utilizes some type of high-tech illuminated skin panels, which endow the craft with chameleon-like characteristics that enable it to blend in with the surrounding sky.

But despite its stealth attributes, the Bird of Prey, or any variation of it, is clearly not a replacement for the SR-71. It utilizes a different, less powerful engine than those used on the SR-71, and therefore a different fuel—flying at a reported maximum speed of only about 300 miles per hour. Still, if the Bird of Prey operated successfully for several years without public knowledge, what other types of shadowcraft are flying that we have not yet heard about?

The information in this article barely scratches the surface of what is known or suspected about stealth technology. But it does, I believe, clearly demonstrate that new and highly advanced aircraft are being developed, and that these aircraft can be mistaken for UFOs. To be sure, it is likely that stealth aircraft are often meant to be mistaken for UFOs, since the phenomenon—whatever it really is—provides a convenient operational smoke screen or camouflage.

What this all comes down to is that mysterious objects seen in the sky need not be something alien or extraterrestrial. They also need not be dimensional/time travelers, optical illusions or mistaken natural phenomena. Instead, some of them just might be secret high-tech aircraft flown by mere mortals such as you and I.

Is There an Underwater UFO Base off the Southern California Coast?
By Preston Dennett

February 2006

Shortly after I began investigating UFOs in the late 1980s, I started to receive reports of unidentified ocean-going craft. Most of these reports came from a certain stretch of California coastline, from about Santa Barbara south to Long Beach. This particular body of water, I soon learned, had a widespread reputation as a UFO hotspot. After several witnesses told me they believed there was an underwater UFO base there, I decided to conduct a more in-depth investigation to determine the truth.

My first step was to survey the research of other prominent investigators. To my surprise, most of the local researchers were already aware of the sightings. Longtime paranormal researcher and author Ann Druffel writes, "This body of water lies between the coastlines of Southern California and Santa Catalina Island, 20 miles offshore to the southwest. The area has for at least thirty years been the scene of UFO reports of all kinds: surface sightings of hazy craft which cruise leisurely in full view of military installations, aerial spheres bobbing in oscillating flight, gigantic cloud-cigars, and at least one report of an underwater UFO with uniformed occupants."

Another researcher, Robert Stanley, editor of the now-defunct magazine *Unicus*, writes, "Even in the Sixties, families were going down to the beach and waiting for a UFO to pass by.... By the 1970s, whole families were going down to the beach at Point Dume at night to watch the multicolored UFOs [that] would sink under the water at times."

MUFON field investigator Bill Hamilton writes, "For years witnesses have seen many types of UFO cruising off the Palos Verdes Peninsula in Southern California. UFOs have actually been seen to come out of the water in the San Pedro Channel."

I had already uncovered several firsthand cases myself. My next step was to put together a comprehensive list of all the recorded ocean-going encounters in the area. I came up with more than 50 sightings. These cases were next categorized into different types.

Coastal Sightings

The most common type of cases take place over the coast-line. In these cases, people see UFOs either from the shore-line or while they are out at sea. What follows are several typical cases.

1953: Engineer Frederick Hehr and several others are on Santa Monica beach when they observe a "squadron of saucers" performing maneuvers in the daylight sky over the bay. Later that day, the objects return and perform more maneuvers for a period of about ten minutes.

July 10, 1955: Around 11:00 a.m., several fishermen off the coast of Newport Beach observe a bluish-silver, cigar-shaped object flying overhead at a "moderate speed and medium altitude." Two and a half hours later, a Washington family of three are sailing 13 miles off the coast of Newport Beach on their way to Catalina Island when they observe a "perfectly round, gray-white" craft about 2,500 feet above their boat. When the object maintains its position over their boat, they radio the Coast Guard, which sends out a plane. The object darts away before the plane arrives.

November 6, 1957: Early morning in Playa Del Rey, three cars driving along the Pacific Coast Highway suddenly stall when a large "egg-shaped object" surrounded in a "blue haze" lands on the beach only a few yards away.

Witnesses Richard Kehoe, Ronald Burke, and Joe Thomas exit their cars and observe two strange-looking men disembarking from the object. The UFO occupants have "yellowish-green skin" and wear "black leather pants, white belts and light colored jerseys." They walk up to the witnesses and begin asking questions. Kehoe and the others are unable to understand the occupants, who are apparently speaking a foreign language. After a few moments, the figures return to the object, which takes off and accelerates out of sight.

That same day at 3:50 p.m., an officer and 12 airmen from an Air Force detachment in nearby Long Beach observe six saucer-shaped objects zooming across the sky. Two hours later, officers at Los Alamitos Naval Air Station report seeing "numerous" objects crisscrossing the sky. At the same time, police stations in Long Beach receive more than 100 calls from residents reporting UFOs.

December 1957: The crew of the British steamship Ramsey observes a large metallic gray disk with antenna-like projections off the coast of San Pedro. One of the crewmen grabs his camera and captures a blurry photo of the object before it moves away.

1960: Actor Chad Everett and two friends are on the rooftop of his Beverly Hills home one night when they observe a lighted object moving back and forth at high speeds over the nearby ocean. Because the object moves so quickly and at right angles, the witnesses are convinced it is a genuine UFO.

1970: As investigated by Bill Hamilton, an anonymous gentleman sailing from Catalina Island to San Pedro Harbor observes a metallic saucer with four "hemispherical pods" underneath it flying only a few hundred feet above his boat.

May 1973: Art director George Gray (pseudonym) observes an object sending down a beam of light while driving along the Pacific Coast Highway in Santa Monica in the pre-dawn hours: "The UFO was over where the beach was ... hovering I would say maybe a hundred, two hundred feet in the air. It was silver. It was your basic UFO ... it was definitely completely metallic with a silver dome on top and a silver dome on the bottom of it, like two plates put together. And it had little lights around it." Gray is able to bring in additional witnesses before the object moves away.

Summer 1988: Professional photographer Kim Carlsberg observes a darting, star-like object while relaxing in her Malibu beachfront home. Suddenly, the object moves directly toward her. "The brilliant point of light advanced until it became a luminous sphere some fifty feet in diameter," reports Carlsberg. "It ominously hung in the air a hundred feet from my window ... the apparent standoff lasted no more than a minute before the sphere departed as quickly as it appeared. It tore away diagonally through the night sky and vanished."

Summer 1990: Private pilot Toshi Inouye and his student observe a large, red, glowing cigar-shaped object hovering near their plane as they fly over the Santa Monica Bay in late afternoon. "It was standing still in the air, glowing red," says Inouye. "We were kind of stunned. We didn't know what to do." Inouye considers calling the nearby airport control tower when the object suddenly darts away.

May 4, 1990: Early in the morning, two Malibu surfers are lying on their surfboards waiting for the next wave when they observe a "brushed aluminum saucer with a bump in the middle [which] approached the shoreline from out of the fog bank sitting about a mile offshore." The object darts back and forth then moves back out to sea.

1998: Adam (pool-cleaner) and Mario (military private) are driving along the Pacific Coast Highway in Malibu when they see six black, diamond-shaped objects darting at high speed up and down the coast. The two men are so impressed by the brief sighting that they spend the next hour driving up and down the coast hoping for a repeat appearance. While they don't see any more UFOs, they do find other UFO watchers. Says Adam, "We did come across a couple of people who were just sitting in their lawn chairs along the road. I don't know if this has anything to do with it, but they were just sitting there along the side of the road, just looking up."

January 3, 2004: Young Chyren is standing along the Santa Monica coast at midday when he observes a metallic, saucer-shaped craft hovering only a few thousand feet directly above a small yacht less than a mile out at sea. He quickly grabs his camera and snaps a photograph.

Into the Ocean

From the reports cited above, it should be clear that UFOs are witnessed over this coastal area in disproportionately large numbers. In most cases, they are observed a few thousand feet or less above the surface of the ocean. It is therefore plausible to speculate that these craft may be traveling into and out of this body of water.

As we shall see, the next category involves UFOs that have been observed doing exactly that. These much more rare cases provide further evidence of an underwater UFO base off the California coast.

November 21, 1951: As reported by researcher Harold Wilkins, several witnesses observe "an unidentified burning object" descending into the ocean somewhere off the coast of California.

August 8, 1954: The Japanese steamship Aliki is off the coast of Long Beach when several members of the crew observe an underwater UFO. As the intercepted radio message from the ship reads, "Saw fireball move in and out of sea without being doused. Left wake of white smoke; course erratic; vanished from sight."

1955: Residents from the northern California coastal town of Santa Maria observe a "long silvery object" emerging from the ocean and taking off into space.

January 15, 1956 (evening): Residents of Redondo Beach report seeing a large, glowing object glide down out of the sky and float on the surface of the ocean about 75 yards off shore.

Dozens of witnesses converge on the scene, including a local night watchman, Redondo Beach lifeguards, and police officers from adjacent Hermosa Beach. As the crowd gathers, the water around the object starts to "froth" and the UFO sinks beneath the surface. The glow of the object, however, remains so intense that it can still be seen.

Police officers radio for assistance and divers are brought in to investigate. Unfortunately, by the time the divers arrive, the object is gone. Another police officer tests the area with a Geiger counter, which fails to register any radiation. Another search the next day also yields no results.

February 9, 1956: Military personnel observe a fireball descending into the ocean off the coast of Redondo Beach.

One year later, UFO researcher Leonard Stringfield obtains an official report on the incident, which says only: "Fireball hits water. Submerges."

July 28, 1962: The captain of a chartered fishing boat notices lights floating in a stationary position in the water about six miles south of Catalina Island. Upon closer observation, the captain is startled to see what he assumes at first is a Russian sub: "It appeared to be the stern of a submarine," he says. "We could see five men, two in white garb, two in dark trousers and white shirts, and one in a sky-blue jump suit. We passed abeam at about a quarter mile and I was certain it was a submarine low in the water, steel gray, no markings, decks almost awash, with only its tail and an odd aft-structure showing."

Suddenly the submarine heads straight for the fishing boat as if to ram it. The captain makes an emergency turn as the sub moves past them at high speed, emitting no noise and leaving no wake except for a "good-sized swell." The captain contacts the navy, which is unable to positively identify the sub.

UFO researchers Coral and Jim Lorenzen hear about the case and speculate that it may have been a UFO and not a submarine: "The high speed, lack of wake and sound, and the huge swell make this object suspect." One might also mention the odd shape of the submarine itself, its lack of fear of observation, and its aggressive maneuvering.

February 5, 1964: Eleven passengers are rescued by the Coast Guard from their emergency raft following the unexplained sinking of their yacht, the Hattie D. The crew was sailing south down the coast of California from Seattle,

Washington, when their yacht either struck or was rammed by an unidentified "metal object." Crewman Carl Jansen says, "I don't care how deep it was...what holed us was steel, and a long piece. There was no give at all."

December 2, 1965: Mrs. Irwin Cohen and her son observe a glowing red object descending into the sea off San Pedro, setting off a large cloud of steam. As the object descends, the witnesses snap a few photos. They wonder if they witnessed a Navy missile or some other unknown object.

October 1968: George Hiner is fishing in his boat off the eastern end of Catalina Island when he spots a "white-domed shaped object" (sic) through his binoculars. As he watches, the object rises ten feet above the surface of the water, then descends and rises again. He notices a strange parachute-like device beneath the object, which gently descends and then sinks beneath the waves.

June 1980: Therapist Linda Susan Young and a friend are driving along the Pacific Coast Highway in Santa Monica at night when Young observes an unusually bright light floating in place several miles out to sea. Young was puzzled by its appearance and turned to tell her friend: "I said to the guy with me, 'What do you suppose this is?' And he turned around and looked at it. And he only saw it for a second when it just shot straight up in the air and blinked out. It didn't look like it went far enough to disappear from view, like a distance. It just sort of stopped. It just stopped being there...I have always assumed it was a UFO."

1980s: An anonymous gentleman (a senior electronics engineer) sailing on a foggy day between Santa Barbara

Island and Santa Cruz Island observes a "fluorescent green colored light" ahead of him in the mist. Thinking it was another ship using bright lights to navigate the fog, he stops and waits for it to pass. As it approaches, however, he is still unable to distinguish any detail. When it is a quarter mile away and heading directly toward him, the witness discovers why: "I finally realized that this dumb thing was underwater... I'm guessing it was—I don't know—maybe 300 feet in diameter, but I couldn't get any vertical dimension on it because it was under me in the water. It literally passed directly underneath me."

The witness is sailing a fully equipped, 38-foot sailboat. As the object passes beneath him, he takes several readings from the depth sounder, determining that the object is about 100 feet deep. At this point, both depth sounders quit functioning. The witness checks his compasses. "All three of them were slowly rotating and I wasn't... I tried calling the Coast Guard and the radio was dead."

The object moves away and disappears, leaving the witness badly frightened. A later check on his equipment reveals that all the compass mountings were broken. Says the witness of the incident, "It was weird. I was just too damned petrified to move."

Underwater Lights

1990: According to investigator Bill Hamilton, starting in late 1989 numerous witnesses in Marina Del Rey begin to have repeated encounters with "strange blue-green lights in the water." As Hamilton writes, "In 1989 and again in 1990, witnesses have seen as many as twenty events an hour.

One large light appeared to be as much as 100 feet in diameter. This large light spawned babies no larger than 10 to 12 feet in length. These lights were seen to move swiftly under the ocean's surface some 500 to 1000 feet from the coastline in Abalone Cove ... one of the lights was reported to have emerged from the water."

Spring 1991: In the early morning hours, Tony X. looks out the window of his Malibu beachfront home and observes a brilliantly lit object floating on the ocean's surface about two miles away. "It looked like a big prism," says Tony, "kind of various colors out there. I got a telescope out there and looked at it." After a few hours, the light winks out.

Two years later, in January 1993, the object returns. "I got the telescope out and looked at it, and it was the same kind of thing ... the colors seemed so pure for lack of a better word. They seemed real coherent." Tony calls up the Coast Guard, but they deny having any information.

May 5, 1992: Two friends walking along Malibu Beach observe a "sort of light/fireball" descend from the sky and into the ocean. Says one witness, "It was going at an incredible speed and it was less than a mile away. It looked like it hit the ocean .... Once the object made its way to the ocean's surface, it disappeared, so my guess is that it went underwater."

1994: Two men walking near the coast of Rancho Palos Verdes at night see several "glowing disks" floating in the water. One of the witnesses returns at a later date and sees the disks again. On this occasion, he observes several black helicopters in the area. Later, he is confronted by unnamed individuals (men in black?) who tell him in no uncertain terms that this area, off Abalone Cove, is off-limits.

January 11, 2002: An anonymous gentleman camping along the coast at Point Mugu sees a light moving back and forth 100 feet above the water, and two other lights beneath the surface of the sea. The objects dart back and forth in tandem for 30 minutes (moving unlike any plane or helicopter), giving the witness the impression that they are searching for something. Afterwards, the light in the sky accelerates out of sight and the two objects in the water dive down and disappear.

Inside the Base

So much underwater UFO activity in one place is undeniably unusual and strongly points to the possibility that there is an underwater UFO base somewhere in this area. While the above reports alone provide considerable evidence, further confirmation of this possibility comes from another source.

Not only is there an unusually large number of sightings, landings, and ocean-going UFOs here, there are also cases of abductions. Normally, when somebody reports being abducted by aliens, they claim to have been taken inside a UFO. However, in this particular area, some abductees report that they have been taken to what is apparently an underground base. Could it be that these witnesses were taken into the underwater base in the Santa Catalina channel?

1967: Two 11-year-old boys experience an episode of missing time while on their parents' boat in Avalon Harbor, Catalina Island. Years later, one of the witnesses, Paul

Nelson (pseudonym) goes under hypnosis and recalls that he and his friend were abducted to an apparently underground base where they were examined by praying-mantis-type ETs: "I was taken into a round-walled room. It seemed to me more underground than it did onboard a ship. The walls had kind of a rock-like facet to them ... rock-like walls rather than craft-type walls. It gave the impression that I was in a cavern [rather] than a ship ... it was more of an underground feeling ... ."

Following the examination, the boys are returned to the boat with no conscious memory of the abduction.

Early 1990s: As recounted in her autobiographical book Beyond My Wildest Dreams, Kim Carlsberg experiences a series of UFO abductions from her Malibu home starting in the early 1990s. On each occasion she is examined by Grey or praying mantis–type ETs.

On August 30, 1992, Carlsberg recalls being taken to what appears to be a vast underground complex where she sees many other abductees and ETs of various types. " ... I woke up in a lobby where many humans were milling around. They reminded me of patients waiting to endure their turns in a dentist's chair." Carlsberg also recalled sitting in a large "auditorium" with many other abductees where she was told by the ETs that she was being "prepared for something."

Hundreds of UFOs

A final piece of evidence for an underwater or underground base comes from the Topanga Canyon UFO wave of 1992 though 1994.

Topanga Canyon has been a UFO hotspot for more than 50 years. However, on the night of June 14, 1992, hundreds of unidentified craft were seen in the canyon, which is situated along the Southern California coast. Seventeen adult witnesses have independently reported seeing UFOs on that evening. One couple, living high on a ridge overlooking the ocean, observed approximately 200 craft rising up, one by one, from behind the ridge east of them, and then moving to various locations in the canyon. As one of the witnesses said, "You know when you watch something for a while... you can figure out where they're coming from? After watching them, you got the feeling that they were going all over this area from that certain spot right there."

That certain spot is the same location where so many underwater UFOs have been seen. And what makes this particular sighting so important is that the objects were not seen coming from above. Instead, these 200 craft came from below, either underground or underwater. Where else could so many UFOs come from except for some kind of base?

Conclusions

As can be seen, the evidence is pretty strong that there is an underwater UFO base in the Santa Catalina channel. Hundreds of UFOs have been seen in the area. A significant portion of these cases involve objects going into and out of the water. And there are cases where people have apparently been taken inside this very base.

It's hard to say exactly where this base is, but judging from the geographic distribution of encounters, the highest density of cases is along the Santa Catalina channel. It would have to be very deep to avoid detection.

The size of the base is again a matter of speculation, but because of the large number of UFOs that have been seen at one time and from the reports of the abductees, it seems safe to assume that this base is extremely large, perhaps the size of several city blocks or more.

How long has this base been here?

The modern age of UFOs began in 1947, when a huge wave of sightings swept across the United States and the world. This was the year of the famous Kenneth Arnold sighting and the alleged UFO crash at Roswell. That year also featured a strange mystery off the California coast.

It began on July 7, 1947, just days after the Roswell crash. At 3:10 p.m., two teenagers walking along the beach at San Raphael watched as a "flat, glistening object" emerged from the ocean, flew for a short distance, then dove back into the water 400 yards from shore.

One month later, in August 1947, the Coast Guard received reports of a "strange flaming object," which fell into the sea.

Following this incident, steamers going into and out of San Francisco Bay encountered an "undersea mountain" that appeared and disappeared in various locations in the bay. Several ships reported the mysterious mass, calling it a "reef" or "submarine mountain" that had apparently appeared overnight. Another ship reported "a large mass under water, off the Golden Gate." Following that, the mass disappeared.

Or perhaps it just moved again. Around this time, the naval survey ship Maury and other craft were sent to investigate another report of a "phantom reef" that had appeared about 400 miles off the coast of Southern California. No charts listed any such mass in the area. And when Captain Hambling of the Maury arrived, the "mass" was gone. The crew immediately surveyed the surrounding area and, to their shock, they found that the mass had moved again. Says Hambling, "Our echo sounders did pick up a strange echo when we were about three-quarters of a mile off the reported location of the 'reef.' It seemed that the sounders had got an echo from a mass about 1,600 yards away. We changed course, and started right towards it. Four hundred yards away from it, we found it had vanished, and we got no other echo. We tracked and re-tracked the area, using fathometers and echo sounders. We covered five square miles very carefully, and another five miles round the outside of the area."

The "mass" however, had gone. Or perhaps it had moved and found a more permanent residence closer to shore. Considering the huge number of underwater reports that started in the 1950s, this may have been the time when the alleged base was constructed. In any case, underwater UFOs have been encountered in this area starting in 1947 and continuing to the present day.

While it may seem hard to believe that ETs are living beneath our oceans, these types of accounts have turned up all over the world. Ocean-going UFOs have been seen in all of the seven seas, reaching back nearly a thousand years and continuing to the present day. With their ability to travel through the oceans and skies with ease, these cases show just how advanced the visitors are. Remember, most of our oceans remain unexplored—at least by humans.

The Invasion Was Televised
By Kenn Thomas

June 2008

The release of Oliver Stone's movie *JFK* in 1991 reminded many of the national brouhaha brought on by Jim Garrison's 1968 investigation of John F. Kennedy's assassination and taught many others about it for the first time. Stone's movie carefully notes that Garrison believed the man he wound up prosecuting, New Orleans businessman Clay Shaw, represented only a toehold on a much larger conspiracy. Among the other players in the crime that Garrison never had enough on to bring to court was a man named Fred Lee Crisman. Garrison had Crisman pegged as one of the trigger men on the grassy knoll. Although the details of this aspect of the Garrison prosecution remain obscure for most, those alive when Garrison's case grabbed national headlines knew Crisman better than they thought they did. Since the fall of 1967, they had watched fictionalized adventures from his life weekly in the form of a science fiction program called *The Invaders*.

At least that's how Crisman saw it. To many, Crisman came off as a scurrilous publicity hound and a teller of tall tales. Nevertheless, the verifiable facts about Crisman's life make his possible connection to *The Invaders* the least of the biographical stories he could embellish for publicity.

Crisman had witnessed the earliest flying saucer sighting of the postwar UFO era, three days before Kenneth Arnold's famous Mount Rainier sightings in 1947. Known as the Maury Island incident, it involved several spinning discs that spewed a weird substance over the shore near Puget Sound, and Arnold was later hired (by FATE co-founder Ray Palmer) to investigate it. The Air Force sent in two investigators as well, and they died in a plane crash trying to bring the substance in for tests.

Weird History

Crisman's connection to both UFOs and the Kennedy assassination is strange enough, especially considering claims that JFK was killed because he was going to expose the Roswell crash. Roswell happened a month after the Maury Island incident. Some researchers think that Roswell, Maury Island, and Arnold's Mount Rainier sightings might all involve the same craft.

Serious JFK scholars usually tangle up the assassination in a tapestry of anti-Castro Cubans, Mafia figures, and the CIA, and try to stay clear of the alien connection for the sake of already shaky credibility issues. Of course, credibility issues surrounded the Maury Island case early on.

The chief witness at Maury Island was a man named Harold Dahl, who worked with Fred Crisman salvaging runaway logs in a harbor patrol boat. Dahl later claimed it was all a hoax. Many UFO researchers have dismissed it that way ever since, even though the slightest review of the historical records shows that Dahl made that claim only after his business was sabotaged, his son kidnapped, and his wife threatened. Dahl suffered an early visit from the infamous Men in Black and was told to keep quiet about what he saw. Thereafter, Dahl declared it all a hoax.

Crisman himself may not have seen anything at all. He visited Maury Island a day after Dahl's sighting and claimed he saw a single saucer on his own. Dahl had multiple witnesses to his sighting as well as physical evidence: the mysterious substance spewed by the saucers killed his dog and injured his son's arm.

Dahl reported the incident to Crisman, whom he regarded as his boss in the lumber-salvaging business. Crisman later went out to the site on his own, to make sure Dahl and the others had not simply gotten drunk and wrecked the boat, and had his sighting without any other witnesses.

Nevertheless, when the Air Force finally sent its investigators, it was Crisman who gave them a Kellogg's Corn Flakes box filled with substances left behind by the UFO at Maury Island. The box and its contents went up in flames, along with the two airmen, when the plane crashed, leading some to suspect that Crisman may have even sabotaged the plane.

According to the most fanciful speculation, Crisman may have kept control of the alien substance to use as blackmail to stay employed in the covert world, even to get choice assignments like the JFK hit. His involvement with Maury Island may have had to do with covering up top-secret radar-fogging discs or the dumping of nuclear waste from the nearby Hanford plutonium reactor. Or he may have been holding on to proof of an extraterrestrial invasion, threatening to expose it to the world if he didn't get what he wanted from the world of spooks and spies.

Secret Knowledge of UFOs

Crisman wanted people to believe that last scenario. In early 1968, he corresponded with well-known UFO researcher Lucius Farish as the contact person for a group he called Parapsychology Research, under the pseudonym Fred Lee. The alias, which only dropped his last name, provided Crisman with a means to discuss himself in the third person, telling Farish: "Mr. Crisman is probably the most informed man in the United States on UFOs and also one of the hardest to find—as the FBI has learned several times."

Crisman presented himself as a man with secret knowledge of UFOs, on the run from the government. In real life, Jim Garrison was on Crisman's heels at that time as a suspect in JFK's murder. In the same letter, Crisman notes: "An interesting fact—one of our members sent a copy of one of the current TV series, 'The Aliens' [sic—*The Invaders*]. It was my understanding that Mr. Crisman was not disturbed or angry, as few things seem to disturb him." Implicitly, though, he experienced a shock of recognition.

In late August 1967, a letter signed by Harold Dahl was sent to UFO researcher Gary Leslie about the show, although this letter too was probably penned by Crisman: "There is a TV series running now that I swear is based in the main on the life of F. Lee Crisman. I know him better than any living man and I know of some of the incredible adventures he has passed through in the last twenty years. I do not mean that his life has been that of this TV hero on the 'Invaders' show ... but there are parts of it that I swear were told to me years ago by Mr. Crisman ... and I know of several that are too wild to be believed ... even by the enlightened attitude of 1967."

The star of *The Invaders*, Roy Thinnes, still makes the rounds of the ufological lecture and conference circuit, bringing hard-to-find episodes of the classic series for showing and offering behind-the-scenes commentary. I caught up with him in Roswell, New Mexico, and gave him a copy my book, Maury Island UFO, the only book ever written on this topic. I explained to Thinnes the connection to the JFK assassination. It was the first he had heard of it. He was unaware if any of the show's scripts had been back-channeled from the field reports of a covert agent, although the show's production company, Quinn-Martin, also produced a series entitled The FBI, based on true cases. The real FBI had final say over that series' cast, and one its technical advisers, Mark Felt, later confessed to being the "Deep Throat" of Watergate fame.

Science Fiction Nightmare

Because Harold Dahl put out the idea that the Maury Island UFO was a hoax, ufologists and the mainstream press gave the story very little play. Kenneth Arnold discussed it in his book *Coming of the Saucers*, and Air Force investigator Edward Ruppelt presented the case in his Report on Unidentified Flying Objects, with changed names and some focus on the Air Force personnel who died. By and large, however, Maury Island flies under the radar of even the most fanatic UFO enthusiasts.

The Maury Island incident made one significant appearance in popular culture, in a comic book by a publisher that also published four issues of a comic book based on The Invaders.

Critics will take obvious swipes at the TV and comic book approach to the JFK assassination. To do that, though, they must overlook those aspects of JFK's death that make it seem like a real-life science fiction nightmare. Jim Garrison believed that Fred Crisman worked as a hired assassin for the military-industrial complex, specifically for Boeing in Seattle. The last speech that JFK made had to do with a defense contract he had given to General Dynamics over Boeing in a highly controversial decision. The contract had to do with the TFX tactical fighter, which later became the F-111 and was sold to the Australians, creating a funding corridor that led to the development of Pine Gap, considered Australia's Area 51.

Consider as well Lee Harvey Oswald, who served at the Atsugi airbase in Japan out of which flew the U-2 spy plane. After Oswald's defection to the Soviet Union, the Soviets had information enough to shoot down Gary Powers's U-2. Before Oswald went to work for the book depository in Dallas, he worked for a firm that processed U-2 film. The U-2 was developed at Area 51.

With all of these often-ignored facts, a dispassionate observer will not be quick to dismiss Crisman's claims or refuse to consider how the JFK assassination may link up with the history of UFOs in modern America.

60 Years of UFO Research
By Brad Steiger

April 2007

On August 3, 2006, the Arkansas Times carried a feature article with the intriguing headline, "UFOs are not what you think."

It turns out that the revelation disclosing the true identity of UFOs is from Terry James of Benton, Arkansas, who has written a novel entitled *The Rapture Dialogues: Dark Dimension*, wherein UFOs are controlled by fallen angels who have incredible powers that can only be thwarted by fundamentalist Christians. *The Rapture Dialogues* is undoubtedly inspired by the enormous success of the Left Behind series of Christian thrillers authored by Religious Right leader Tim LaHaye and Jerry Jenkins.

Combining UFOs with the Rapture, the arrival of the Antichrist, the approach of Armageddon, and the return of Jesus is really not a new concept to readers of FATE. And while many UFO researchers may become impatient with this approach to the UFO enigma, millions of Christian evangelicals and fundamentalists agree with the premise that the mysterious signs in the sky herald the end times.

Indeed, a growing number of UFO theorists now wonder if perhaps the flying saucer phenomenon may be somehow tied into an approaching doomsday.

From George Adamski onward, flying saucer contactees have passed along stern warnings from the Space Brothers that humankind must stop its primitive warlike ways and prepare for a coming physical evolution and a spiritual elevation in consciousness.

New Age adherents have also begun to weave doomsday scenarios. Currently, a number of channelers are relaying messages from Count St. Germain advising us to prepare for the end times, and others interpret the Mayan calendar as declaring the end of our world sometime in the year 2012. And always, these prophetic visions proclaim, the entities associated with UFOs stand ready to assist earthlings during these times of dramatic transitions.

While some UFO investigators are pondering the links between UFOs and ancient texts predicting a fast-approaching Armageddon, others are resisting an increasing amount of evidence that such landmark UFO "proofs" as the Roswell crash (1947), the Socorro sighting (1964), and many others were, indeed, our own secret craft jump-started by the 1,600 German scientists smuggled into the United States during Operation Paperclip at the close of World War II. Shunning such conspiracies of silence by the government as evidence that the flying saucers of the late 1940s were experimental craft of our own Earth scientists, a number of diehard UFO researchers continue their efforts to prove that alien spacecraft and their crews come from outer space. Incredible amounts of energy are expended in the UFO community by internecine quarrels over the validity of government documents, alien autopsies, and deathbed disclosures from high-ranking military figures who claimed to have seen alien bodies and held fragments of crashed alien vehicles.

We've Learned Nothing

Any observer of the UFO scene had to sense new attitudes and theories within the field when James W. Moseley, who founded S.A.U.C.E.R.S.—the Saucer and Unexplained Celestial Events Research Society—in July 1954, postulated in a 1998 issue of his newsletter *Saucer Smear* the rhetorical question of what Great Truths he had learned about UFOs in four decades of research: "The answer," he responded, "is none."

Noted for his satirical sense of humor, Moseley became uncharacteristically serious when he stated that his current view of the UFO mystery was that it is just one of a vast spectrum of unexplained events that seemed to be unsolvable, "but which should convince us that this Universe is a much more complex place than most people have ever imagined."

Continuing in a philosophical vein, Moseley said that one reason why UFO researchers will never solve the mystery "is because it is interrelated with the most fundamental mysteries of human life: Where did we come from? Why are we here? Where, if anywhere, do we go next? These questions can be answered through religious faith, but seem to be well beyond present-day science. Possibly UFOs come from other planets, but it is much more likely that they are a part of the Earth's environment—whatever that means. Even the so-called 'Government Cover-Up' has never been properly documented as to its extent and purpose or even to its existence."

After 60 years of serious investigation, we UFO researchers can't even agree among ourselves if the enigma originates from outer space or within ourselves—or if it is some metaphysical combination of the two.

An Increasingly Complex Problem

In its beginnings, UFO research was so much simpler. Mysterious objects and lights were sighted in the sky in 1947, and one of the popularly named "flying saucers" allegedly crashed near Roswell, New Mexico. The Army Air Force acknowledged that they possessed fragments of the wreckage—then officially announced that the crash pieces were from a weather balloon, not an extraterrestrial vehicle. Thus began accusations of a government cover-up, and when such respected individuals as retired Marine Maj. Donald Keyhoe told us that the flying saucers were real and from outer space, we believed them. The challenge placed before all UFO researchers was to collect data and evidence to prove to a skeptical public that the flying saucers originated in some faraway planet or universe.

In 1966, when I was promoting my first UFO book, *Strangers from the Skies*, I devised what I thought was a clever retort for all those hostile media interviewers who asked me, "Come on, do you really believe in flying saucers?"

"No," I responded, "I don't believe in UFOs. I believe in God. The reality that flying saucers exist and are invading our skies has nothing at all to do with belief."

When I wrote *Strangers from the Skies*, I was as "nuts-and-bolts" an advocate of physical craft and crews visiting our planet from an extraterrestrial source as any of the other researchers and writers of that era of UFO investigation.

As I got deeper into researching the UFO phenomenon, traveling across the United States and Canada to alleged landing sites, speaking with witnesses who claimed to have had close encounters with aliens, and interviewing contactees and abductees, bizarre, paraphysical occurrences that seemed to belong more in the arena of psychic phenomena began to happen all around me. Contactees began to sound more like spirit mediums and seemed to be spouting a kind of cosmic gospel. Individuals who had experienced close encounters reported eerie activities in their homes that sounded more like poltergeist activity than the actions of extraterrestrial aliens exploring our planet. All of these UFO manifestations were beginning to seem more likely the result of explosions of psychic phenomena rather than byproducts of an alien invasion. I had no doubt that something unusual, something very special, had occurred to these men and women—but what?

On numerous occasions I heard abductees tell about their having been taken up through ceilings, out through walls, levitated out windows, and taken to an extraterrestrial world or an alien medical laboratory. In his second letter to the Corinthians, the apostle Paul confides that he was once taken up into Heaven. But even in an age far more tolerant of supernatural occurrences and far less exacting in its scientific requirements than our own, the epistle writer provides a number of qualifying statements that many of our contemporary UFO abductees would do well to emulate:

"Fourteen years ago, I was taken up to Heaven for a visit. Don't ask me whether my body was there or just my spirit, for I don't know; only God can answer that. But anyway, there I was in paradise and heard things so astounding that they are beyond a man's power to describe or put into words (and anyway, I am not allowed to tell them to others). That experience is something worth bragging about, but

I am not going to do it" (2 Corinthians 12:2–5, Catholic One Year Bible).

As an investigator, I had to be open to the possibility that these individuals were having genuine encounters with physical beings from other material worlds. I tried to listen to such accounts in an objective manner, but I wondered if these occurrences might not really be reports of personal mystical experiences that had taken place in dreams, visions, or out-or-body experiences. My extensive study of paranormal phenomena had convinced me that it is possible for the human essence to soar free of the accepted limitations of time and physical space imposed upon it by the material body and to engage in astral travels. An abductee's account of being taken aboard a UFO might actually be descriptions of a spiritual, nonmaterial experience, rather than an actual physical, material one.

By the early 1970s, I had reached the conclusion that UFOs, ghosts, poltergeists, revelatory experiences, and even seemingly misplaced archaeological anomalies were all facets of some larger intelligent, teaching mechanism. In *Gods of Aquarius: UFOs and the Transformation of Man* (1976), I theorized that it didn't matter who among us saw UFOs, because any individual contact with UFO intelligences becomes part of the common experience of all humankind. It also seemed clear to me that the UFOs, the appearances of humanoid entities, and the manifestation of archetypal images throughout the world signified that we were part of a larger community of intelligences, both physical and nonphysical, seen and unseen, than we had been bold enough to believe.

On August 3, 2006, a press release promised that Craig Jacocks would share proof of his alien abduction in his book, *Aware of Their Presence*. While Whitley Strieber's *Communion* became an international bestseller recounting the details of a distasteful physical examination, Jacocks, so we are told, can offer proof that we are not alone. According to Jacocks, a scanner has reacted to an unknown code inside his body and X-rays have revealed needle-like objects that he believes to be tracking devices. Jacocks claims to have been abducted since he was a child when he began hearing alien voices speaking to him.

Researcher John W. White has stated his conclusions that the alien "medical exam" reported by numerous abductees is a sham and a cover for something even more insidious than unwelcome poking and probing: "How many skin samples do alien 'scientists' need before they have sufficient data? Why hasn't their data-gathering become more sophisticated over the decades? ... While performing ... their seemingly elementary examination of abductees, the aliens demonstrate that they have a highly detailed knowledge of human psychology, physiology, and anatomy. Abductee reports show that the aliens can completely control the human nervous system. When the aliens want to abduct them, abductees are routinely paralyzed instantly and placed in suspended animation. I conclude that the alien 'medical exam' is a sham and a cover for brainwashing and mind control."

It has also occurred to numerous researchers that the lurid descriptions of sexual probings aboard a UFO could well be nothing more than a variation of the age-old incubus-succubus phenomenon. In such accounts, semen is extracted from human males by the *succubi* (female demon) and then introduced into human females in *incubi* (male demon) incidents. Early fairy lore is filled with identical cases, and such sexual manipulations are an integral part of witchcraft lore.

White has stated his opinion that there are good and bad aliens, just as there are good and bad people. "Some of them may indeed be motivated by visions and values in keeping with our own most transcendent insights and sacred wisdom," he suggests. "Others, however, are not... If alien abductions are the work of angels, let us be clear about who they are: fallen angels or demonic entities. They are the same intelligences who have been characterized in ancient scriptures and sacred traditions as native to Earth, diabolic, hostile to our very existence, and intent upon dominating us totally—physically, mentally, spiritually."

False Memories

Critical of UFO investigators who use hypnosis to help alleged abductees recall their harrowing experiences, anthropologist Dr. Elizabeth Bird sought to explore other possibilities that might explain the abductees' trauma. Dr. Bird maintains that "while hypnosis may elicit remarkably detailed accounts, they are no more accurate than normal memories. Indeed, suggestible people produce notably less accurate accounts under hypnosis."

The ease with which a false memory could be created was demonstrated by an experiment conducted in 2001 by University of Washington memory researchers Jacquie E. Pickrell and Dr. Elizabeth F. Loftus. About one-third of

120 subjects proved susceptible to the suggestion that they had met Bugs Bunny at Disneyland and had even shaken his hand. Such a scenario could never have taken place in real life, because Bugs is a Warner Brothers cartoon character and would never appear at Disneyland.

Dr. Loftus's extensive research into the various means by which false memories may be created suggests three common methods: yielding to social or professional demands to recall particular events, imagining events when experiencing difficulty remembering, and being encouraged to abandon critical thinking regarding the truth of memory constructs.

Other medical researchers have likened the abduction experience to sleep paralysis, a condition that occurs in that hypnogogic state just before falling asleep or just before fully awakening. Although the condition may only last for a few seconds, during that time a person undergoing sleep paralysis is unable to move or speak and often experiences a sense of fear that there is some unknown presence in the room. Many individuals undergoing the condition report the sensation of being touched or pulled, or feeling a great pressure on the chest. Along with such tactile sensations, the experiencer often has hallucinations and believes that he or she sees ghosts, angels, devils, or extraterrestrial beings.

Folklorist Bill Ellis, assistant professor of English and American Studies at Pennsylvania State University, has cited numerous comparisons between UFO abduction experiences and accounts of the phenomenon known in folk culture as the Old Hag: "A person who is relaxed but apparently awake suddenly finds himself paralyzed in the presence of some nonhuman entity. Often, the sensation is accompanied by terrifying hallucinations—of shuffling sounds, of humanoid figures with prominent eyes. Often the figure even sits on the victim's chest, causing a choking sensation."

Paranormal Is Now Normal

In the *Journal of Nervous and Mental Disease*, psychiatrists Colin Ross of Dallas and Shaun Joshi of Winnipeg state that paranormal experiences are so common in the general population that no theory of normal psychology that does not take them into account can be considered comprehensive.

A growing number of mental health professionals are discovering that people who think that they have seen a UFO or a space alien may be just as intelligent and psychologically healthy as other folks. According to psychologists at Carleton University of Ottawa, Canada, writing in the November 1993 issue of the *Journal of Abnormal Psychology*, "Our findings clearly contradict the previously held notions that people who seemingly had bizarre experiences, such as missing time and communicating with aliens, have wild imaginations and are easily swayed into believing the unbelievable."

Dr. Nicholas P. Spanos, who led the study and administered a battery of psychological tests to a large number of UFO experiencers, said that such people were not at all "off the wall." On the contrary, he affirmed, "They tend to be white-collar, relatively well-educated representatives of the middle class."

In more recent studies, such researchers as Susan A. Clancy, author of *Abducted: How People Come to Believe They Were Kidnapped by Aliens* (2005), also found the abductees to be likeable, seemingly normal individuals—but neverthe-less, personable men and women who were self-delusional.

The decree of open-minded psychologists that one may experience a UFO encounter and not be analyzed as crazy will come as no small comfort to those experiencers of the mystery who have suddenly found themselves enmeshed in a veritable maelstrom of bizarre and unexplainable occur-rences. On the other hand, there is some solace to be gained in learning that we are becoming more and more a nation of mystics.

The January 12, 1994, issue of USA Today presented the results of a survey conducted by Jeffrey S. Levin, associ-ate professor at Eastern Virginia Medical School, Norfolk, Virginia, which stated that more than two-thirds of the U.S. population has undergone at least one mystical experience. Furthermore, Levin notes that while only 5 percent of the populace have such experiences often, "they seem to be get-ting more common with each successive generation." And interestingly, those individuals who are active in church or synagogue report fewer mystical experiences than those in the general population.

Acknowledging that these kinds of experiences have been around "from time immemorial," Levin suggests that the stigma of mental illness or religious accusations of demon possession could have prevented more people from reporting them in earlier times.

Interestingly, on July 22, 2006, ABC Radio National reported that an estimated 10 percent of the population hears voices that aren't there. Some people learn to live harmoniously with these voices and sometimes find them to be spiritually uplifting and comforting.

Seventeen Theories

I have now authored or co-authored 22 books on a wide range of UFO phenomena. Today I answer interviewers' questions regarding my conclusions about the UFO enigma by stating that I believe in the reality of the phenomenon, but I have 17 theories as to what the UFO might be (see www.rense.com/general67/ENIG.HTM). I cringe whenever well-intentioned researchers, abductees, or channelers tell me that they know exactly what UFOs are.

"The thrust of UFO research is into the metaphysical, where things are not always as they seem," researcher John W. White has said.

The dangers and hazards inherent in UFO research were effectively summarized in a story that was sent to me by one of my longtime correspondents, who spotted the account in the daily newspaper of a medium-sized Midwestern city. According to a perplexed, yet fascinated, reporter, a clergyman told her that he had spent the past 23 years running from UFO beings, angels, or aliens. The minister said that he was no longer certain just what the beings were, but he was sure that they were truly from another world or dimension.

According to the clergyman, he had a rather conventional sighting of a UFO, and although he did not report the sighting to anyone other than family and friends, he soon became aware that someone—or something—was following him as he performed his daily ministerial tasks. An uneasy feeling told him that it was some form of intelligence related to the UFO sighting and that it was stalking him. A bizarre series of happenings afflicted the minister wherever he went, leading eventually to the dissolution of his marriage and an extreme difficulty in maintaining a fully functional ministry. In utter confusion, he resigned from his duties with the congregation and left for another city in another state.

For ten years, he worked as a counselor in a halfway house. He had been unable to accept another parish ministry because of the continuing series of weird events that haunted his very existence. On the tenth anniversary of his UFO sighting, "aliens" visited him in his home.

The aliens or whatever they were allowed him to photograph them with his Polaroid camera, and they freely demonstrated their ability to assume whatever physical form they chose. The frightened and astonished minister saw them change shape, glow in the dark, and materialize and dematerialize right in front of him.

Feeling somewhat secure with his photographic proof of the physical reality of the entities, the minister believed that he was now in possession of some kind of cosmic trump card that would somehow keep the things away from him. Suffused also with feelings of vindication, he told a few close friends and members of his family that he now had proof that he was not crazy and had not been making up paranoid stories for the past ten years.

A few days later, three friendly police officers appeared at his home. Explaining that they were sincere UFO buffs, they said they had heard about his remarkable photographs of aliens and they were extremely eager to see them.

Although the minister was surprised that the few people in whom he had confided had broadcast his coup of having obtained snapshots of otherworldly beings, these men, after all, were the police. And they weren't laughing at him. They were very serious when they examined the photographs, and they were firm in their arguments that such solid proof of aliens among human society should be widely published in the media.

The minister was reluctant. He had endured enough ridicule since his initial sighting a decade before. But the sympathetic police officers assured him that they would use their credentials to get the pictures published and to restore his own credibility as a clergyman. Together, they would prove to the world at large that such creatures were walking among humankind.

When the officers arrived on the following night, however, they threatened him, confiscated his photographs, taped his hands behind his back, pulled a stocking cap over his head, and tossed him roughly into the back of a van. After the phony policemen drove him around for a while, loudly discussing whether or not they should kill him, they finally released him in a remote wooded area.

Although the minister felt fortunate that he was still alive, he realized that his proof of alien entities had been taken by the men who had been posing as police officers. A few months later he began to notice strange physical side effects, which he blamed on his close contact with the three policemen—whom he now understood were actually the aliens assuming yet another disguise. The upper portion of his torso became scaly. His vision became blurred, and from time to time he was temporarily blind.

When the journalist interviewed the beleaguered clergyman, he was receiving emotional support from other ministers and praying without ceasing that the UFO beings—the shape-changers, the angels, or the demons—had finally decided to leave him alone.

The Reality Game

The tale of the hapless minister epitomizes in so many ways the bizarre and chaotic psychological and physical nightmares that await careless investigators of the UFO mystery—where things are seldom what they seem.

Whatever we are up against, I believe that both the actors and their eerie scenarios are very, very old. However, each generation of humans is challenged to participate in a seemingly crazy cosmic contest that I have come to label the "Reality Game."

According to Roman Catholic scholar Matthew Fox, the number one cosmological question in the Mediterranean area in the first century AD was whether or not the angels who were being so frequently reported were friends or foes.

With today's maddening melee of accounts of UFO beings on the one hand presenting accurate prophecies, performing miraculous healings, and offering benevolent guidance; and on the other hand participating in cruel abductions, conducting genetic experiments, and plotting our planet's destruction or enslavement, UFO researchers must ask a similar question in the new millennium: Are the UFO beings friends or foes? And we might add, are they from inner or outer space?

Whatever the UFO phenomenon really is, I believe that it has always been an integral aspect of our evolution as a species and I believe that we will continue to have a symbiotic relationship with the UFO as we progress into the future. That being said, I cannot satisfactorily define the precise parameters of the mystery that is the UFO—and I don't believe anyone else can either.

Throughout our species' historical struggle to achieve some level of technological sophistication, the UFO mystery has generally chosen to conduct its activities in disguise. In regard to the phenomenon's motives and overall game plan, it has elected to keep the ultimate goal a secret.

Sometimes it seems as though we are dealing only with caustic tricksters who deliberately seek to confuse us and to mislead us concerning their true purpose on the planet. In other instances, there appear to be dramatic clues that indicate we are dealing with benign paraphysical entities that may have always coexisted with us and who are even now participating with us in some grand evolutionary design. Still other fragments of circumstantial evidence indicate that we are in occasional contact with superscientists from Somewhere who created us and many of the other life forms on this planet and who continually hover over their handiwork, shepherding their biological field project.

In *Mysteries of Time and Space*, I suggested that the beings that we call the UFO intelligences might be working toward our gradual redefining of our concept of reality by challenging us in the teasing fashion of a Zen riddle. We may have been challenged to play the Reality Game; and if we can once apprehend the true significance of the preposterous clues, if we can but master the proper moves, we may obtain a clearer picture of our role in the cosmic scheme of things.

As in UFO research in general, the rules of the Reality Game may be confusing, extremely flexible, and difficult to define, but play we must—for it may be the only game in the Universe.

To Write to the Author

If you wish to contact the author or would like more information about this book, please write to the author in care of Llewellyn Worldwide and we will forward your request. Both the author and publisher appreciate hearing from you and learning of your enjoyment of this book and how it has helped you. Llewellyn Worldwide cannot guarantee that every letter written to the author can be answered, but all will be forwarded. Please write to:

℅ Llewellyn Worldwide
2143 Wooddale Drive
Woodbury, MN 55125-2989, U.S.A.

Please enclose a self-addressed stamped envelope for reply,
or $1.00 to cover costs. If outside the U.S.A., enclose
an international postal reply coupon.